Anxiety Disorders

Peggy J. Parks

Diseases and Disorders

ReferencePoint
Press®

San Diego, CA

© 2011 ReferencePoint Press, Inc.
Printed in the United States

For more information, contact:
ReferencePoint Press, Inc.
PO Box 27779
San Diego, CA 92198
www.ReferencePointPress.com

Picture credits:
Cover: Dreamstime and iStockphoto.com
Maury Aaseng: 31–33, 46–48, 61–62, 75–77
AP Images: 12, 16

LIBRARY OF CONGRESS CATALOGING-IN-PUBLICATION DATA

Parks, Peggy J., 1951–
   Anxiety disorders / by Peggy J. Parks.
     p. cm. — (Compact research series)
   Includes bibliographical references and index.
   ISBN-13: 978-1-60152-137-8 (hardcover)
   ISBN-10: 1-60152-137-5 (hardcover)
   1. Anxiety disorders—Juvenile literature. 2. Phobias—Juvenile literature. I. Title.
   RC531.P37   2011
   616.85'22—dc22

                                      2010031813

Contents

Foreword

66Where is the knowledge we have lost in information?99

—T.S. Eliot, "The Rock."

As modern civilization continues to evolve, its ability to create, store, distribute, and access information expands exponentially. The explosion of information from all media continues to increase at a phenomenal rate. By 2020 some experts predict the worldwide information base will double every 73 days. While access to diverse sources of information and perspectives is paramount to any democratic society, information alone cannot help people gain knowledge and understanding. Information must be organized and presented clearly and succinctly in order to be understood. The challenge in the digital age becomes not the creation of information, but how best to sort, organize, enhance, and present information.

ReferencePoint Press developed the *Compact Research* series with this challenge of the information age in mind. More than any other subject area today, researching current issues can yield vast, diverse, and unqualified information that can be intimidating and overwhelming for even the most advanced and motivated researcher. The *Compact Research* series offers a compact, relevant, intelligent, and conveniently organized collection of information covering a variety of current topics ranging from illegal immigration and deforestation to diseases such as anorexia and meningitis.

The series focuses on three types of information: objective single-author narratives, opinion-based primary source quotations, and facts and statistics. The clearly written objective narratives provide context and reliable background information. Primary source quotes are carefully selected and cited, exposing the reader to differing points of view. And facts and statistics sections aid the reader in evaluating perspectives. Presenting these key types of information creates a richer, more balanced learning experience.

For better understanding and convenience, the series enhances information by organizing it into narrower topics and adding design features that make it easy for a reader to identify desired content. For example, in *Compact Research: Illegal Immigration*, a chapter covering the economic impact of illegal immigration has an objective narrative explaining the various ways the economy is impacted, a balanced section of numerous primary source quotes on the topic, followed by facts and full-color illustrations to encourage evaluation of contrasting perspectives.

The ancient Roman philosopher Lucius Annaeus Seneca wrote, "It is quality rather than quantity that matters." More than just a collection of content, the *Compact Research* series is simply committed to creating, finding, organizing, and presenting the most relevant and appropriate amount of information on a current topic in a user-friendly style that invites, intrigues, and fosters understanding.

Anxiety Disorders at a Glance

Anxiety Disorders Defined

Anxiety disorders all revolve around intense, often overpowering anxiety that is caused by irrational fear and dread.

Types of Anxiety Disorders

The six main types of anxiety disorders are generalized anxiety disorder, social anxiety disorder, panic disorder, obsessive-compulsive disorder, post-traumatic stress disorder, and specific phobias.

Prevalence

Together, anxiety disorders represent the most common form of mental illness in the United States, with more than 40 million American adults suffering from one or more of them.

Causes

Scientists believe that risk factors such as genetics, brain chemistry, personality, and life events work together to cause anxiety disorders.

Effects of Anxiety Disorders

The fear, dread, and physical symptoms associated with anxiety disorders can significantly interfere with one's life and even lead to total incapacitation.

Diagnosis

A trained psychotherapist assesses the patient's anxiety levels in specific situations and evaluates whether there is significant interference with daily life.

Treatment

Numerous mental health professionals say that the most effective treatment for someone with one or more anxiety disorders is a combination of medications and psychotherapy.

Overcoming Anxiety Disorders

People with anxiety disorders have as much as a 90 percent chance of overcoming them if they undergo the right treatment program, but the majority of sufferers never seek treatment.

Overview

❝When anxiety rules, life loses its joy and spontaneity. Everyday activities are fraught with difficulty.❞

—Pamela Wampler, a licensed psychotherapist who has suffered from severe panic attacks.

❝When anxiety becomes an excessive, irrational dread of everyday situations, it has become a disabling disorder.❞

—National Institute of Mental Health, which seeks to reduce mental illness and behavioral disorders through research.

A woman who uses the pseudonym "Merely Me" talks freely about her struggle with anxiety disorders in an online forum. She knows firsthand what it is like to suffer from such extreme anxiety that it interferes with normal daily functioning, and she has struggled with this since she was a child. She writes:

> I was the little girl in grade school who refused to climb down the open metal stairs leading to the playground. I was the teen who refused to dive off the diving board and ended up being pushed into the water as I gasped and struggled so much that the teacher had to hook me out with a pole as my classmates looked on and giggled. I was the girl who went on dates to the amusement park and wouldn't ride anything but the bumper cars.[1]

As the years went by, her anxieties grew, and she continued to be plagued by numerous fears and dread. She explains: "I was the young woman in college who climbed thirty flights of stairs rather than get on the university's rickety elevator. I was the woman who, needing minor surgery, pleaded with the doctor not to kill me. I am the same person . . . who asked the person sitting next to me during a plane ride, 'Are you certain there are no terrorists on this plane?'"[2]

What Are Anxiety Disorders?

The word *anxiety* refers to the worry, apprehension, or fear that humans feel when they are under stress, are faced with real danger, or perceive that they are threatened in some way. This sort of anxiety is perfectly normal and can even be a valuable trait, as clinical psychologist George Pratt writes: "Anxiety is part of the human experience, I'm afraid. It has some productive aspects as well. We know that, with anxiety, we're secreting various stress hormones that cause us to be more alert and awake and aware, and it can serve to help us in dangerous situations such as escape."[3]

For those who suffer from anxiety disorders, however, worry and fear are magnified to the point of interfering with normal functioning and everyday life. For some people these heightened anxieties can be debilitating. As the agency Health Canada explains: "People who suffer from anxiety disorders have long periods of intense feelings of fear or distress out of proportion to real events. Their brains interpret real or imagined events to be much more risky or dangerous than they really are. Their lives are full of unease and fear, which interferes with their personal and professional relationships."[4]

Millions of Sufferers

According to the Anxiety Disorders Association of America, more than 40 million Americans aged 18 and over, and 9 million children, suffer from 1 or more anxiety disorders. The National Institute of Mental Health (NIMH) has identified 6 main types: specific phobias, social anxiety disorder, generalized anxiety disorder, post-traumatic stress disorder (PTSD), panic disorder, and obsessive-compulsive disorder (OCD). Collectively, these disorders represent the most common form of mental illness in the United States.

Although each anxiety disorder has its own traits and symptoms, there is one common thread: they all revolve around excessive, irrational fear. According to the NIMH, specific phobias are the most common. More than 19 million adults have been diagnosed with one or more specific phobias, with women twice as likely to have them as men. Social anxiety disorder, also prevalent among both men and women, affects about 15 million adults, while an estimated 7.7 million American adults suffer from PTSD. About 6.8 million people have generalized anxiety disorder, 6 million have panic disorder, and 2.2 million suffer from OCD.

Living with Fear and Dread

People with generalized anxiety disorder are plagued by exaggerated worry and tension even though little or nothing has happened to provoke the feelings. This extreme anxiety causes them to be jittery and unable to relax, to startle easily, and to have trouble sleeping. A related condition, social anxiety disorder, fills sufferers with fear and dread of any sort of social situation. People with this condition worry that they are constantly being watched or judged, and they live in fear that they will do something to humiliate themselves. A young woman named Amanda shares her thoughts about what it feels like to have social anxiety disorder: "It's like being afraid of the dark because you know nothing's there, but you're still scared of it. It's an irrational fear, and you know it's an irrational fear, but you're still scared and you can't help it."[5]

For those who suffer from anxiety disorders . . . worry and fear are magnified to the point of interfering with normal functioning and everyday life.

Social anxiety disorder is also called social phobia because it involves an intense, irrational fear of any type of social situation. Many other types of phobias exist as well, with people who suffer from them fearing a variety of different objects or situations. Some of the most common are claustrophobia, a fear of confined places such as crowded rooms, closets, elevators, and tunnels; acrophobia, the fear of heights; arachnophobia, the fear of spiders; and aviophobia, the fear of flying in planes. In addition to these common phobias, experts have documented cases of people who react with terror to mirrors, fish, clowns, birds, computer technology, the color red, and even clouds.

New York City journalist Lev Grossman suffers from an unusual phobia: the fear of being around anyone who is eating or drinking. He writes: "Some people are scared of snakes or flying or heights or other things that can actually be dangerous. I'm filled with overpower-
ing, irrational dread by the sight
or sound of another human being
eating or drinking. It doesn't make
any more sense to me than it does
to you. But that's what a phobia is:
a fear that has nothing to do with
logic or common sense."[8]

> " Country music
> superstar Carrie
> Underwood has
> suffered from panic
> attacks since she
> was in high school. "

Irrational fears are also an unfortunate fact of life for people
with panic disorder. Many live with overwhelming terror and feelings of doom, and they are prone to sudden, inexplicable bouts of terror known as panic attacks. These attacks can strike at any time, anyplace, and can last from 10 minutes to a much longer period of time. Country music su-
perstar Carrie Underwood has suffered from panic attacks since she was in high school. She experiences this most often when she is in a crowd, such as at a large, busy store. In an effort to avoid the attacks, Under-
wood shops late at night, when she is less likely to encounter hordes of people. She explains: "I'm horrible in crowds. I just get so nervous. . . . I do not like shopping in close quarters and stuff like that; I just can't do that." Drawing an invisible square around herself, she adds: "This is my space. And I'm really weird about it."[6]

Tormented by the Mind

People with OCD suffer from persistent, upsetting thoughts known as obsessions, and they use ritualistic behaviors (compulsions) in an effort to satisfy the nagging thoughts. As the group OCD Chicago explains:

> Everyone's brain churns out random and strange thoughts. Most people simply dismiss them and move on, but they get "stuck" in the brains of people with OCD. These ran-
> dom thoughts are like the brain's junk mail. Most people have a spam filter and can simply ignore junk mail that

Award-winning country music singer Carrie Underwood says she has suffered from panic attacks since she was in high school. She experiences this most often when she is in a crowd, such as at a large, busy store.

comes their way. But having OCD is like having a spam filter that has stopped working—the junk mail just keeps coming and you cannot make it stop. Soon, the junk mail seriously outnumbers the wanted mail, and you become overwhelmed.[7]

As with all anxiety disorders, OCD symptoms vary based on how severe someone's disorder is. For instance, people with mild forms of OCD may be unable to sleep at night until they check and recheck that all doors are locked, the oven and stove are turned off, and the iron is unplugged. If these acts do not interfere with normal functioning, they are likely not cause for concern. But OCD can be a crippling disorder when someone is constantly haunted by obsessive thoughts and feels powerless to stop them.

Accompanying Disorders

It is common for people with anxiety disorders also to suffer from other illnesses or disorders, as the NIMH explains: "Anxiety disorders commonly occur along with other mental or physical illnesses, including alcohol or substance abuse, which may mask anxiety symptoms or make them worse."[9] Two disorders that are often accompanied by drug abuse or alcoholism are panic disorder and PTSD, as sufferers use mind-altering substances in an attempt to reduce or eliminate their anxiety. The same is true with generalized anxiety disorder, which is often accompanied by substance abuse and/or depression, as well as other anxiety disorders.

One neurological disorder that has been connected with the anxiety disorder OCD is Tourette syndrome. This is a condition that causes patients to have involuntary movements known as tics and to make repetitive noises such as snorting, grunting, and/or screeching. According to Maryland psychologist Charles S. Mansueto, even though OCD and Tourette are two different disorders, substantial evidence from research suggests a close relationship between them. He writes: "The frequent concurrence of symptoms of both disorders in the same individual is one strong clue. Up to 60% of TS [Tourette syndrome] sufferers have been reported to have OCD symptoms, 50% of children with OCD are reported to have had tics and 15% met criteria for TS."[10]

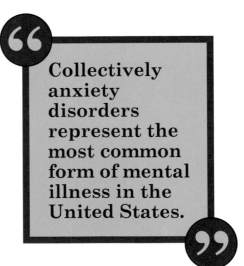

Collectively anxiety disorders represent the most common form of mental illness in the United States.

What Causes Anxiety Disorders?

The cause (or causes) of anxiety disorders is not well understood. It is widely believed that multiple factors are involved, one of which is genetics. As the Anxiety Disorders Association of America states: "Researchers are learning that anxiety disorders run in families, and that they have a biological basis, much like allergies or diabetes and other disorders."[11] The hereditary theory of anxiety disorders has been confirmed in studies with twins. Studies have shown that if an identical twin has one or more anxiety disorders, the second twin has a higher-than-normal likelihood of also having an anxiety disorder.

Genetics alone cannot explain anxiety disorders, however, since many people who are genetically at risk, or predisposed, never develop them. Because of this, researchers suspect that the disorders are the result of genetic predisposition combined with environmental factors. The Anxiety Disorders Association of America explains: "Anxiety disorders may develop from a complex set of risk factors, including genetics, brain chemistry, personality, and life events."[12]

Anxiety Disorder Misconceptions

Because anxiety disorders are widely misunderstood, people often jump to erroneous conclusions about those who suffer from them. For instance, it is often assumed that extreme feelings of anxiousness are imagined, rather than real, and are no different from the anxiety that everyone experiences. Sufferers may be dismissed as hypochondriacs who want people to believe they are suffering as a way of garnering attention for themselves. As psychiatrist Jack M. Gorman writes: "Sometimes these people are even accused of fabricating their symptoms to get attention. Those notions are clearly false."[13]

> **Because anxiety disorders are widely misunderstood, people often jump to erroneous conclusions about those who suffer from them.**

Another erroneous assumption is that people with anxiety disorders could recover if they tried harder. Even friends and family members may lose patience with them, mistakenly assuming that they do not want to get better. As Merely Me writes: "The feelings you have, although others may pooh pooh them, tell you to just 'get over it' or 'buck up' are very real and very physical. And there is genuine suffering with anxiety. There can be a constant beating yourself up for not being able to handle life as others seemingly do with ease."[14]

What Are the Effects of Anxiety Disorders?

Many people with anxiety disorders live with unbearable anguish. Those who have panic disorder, for instance, go from day to day with no idea when or where the next panic attack will occur. This creates a vicious cycle, because the very thought that an attack could strike at any time evokes such an intense sense of dread that it can actually trigger an at-tack. The associated physical effects, such as chest pain, a pounding heart, excessive sweating, dizziness, and even feelings of being suffocated, can be terrifying for the person having the panic attack. Psychiatrist David L. Ginsberg explains: "A panic attack in-volves such a high level of anxiety that the person affected feels as if he or she can't breathe, is having a heart attack, going insane, or losing control."[15]

> " It can be diffi-cult to determine which anxiety disorder or dis-orders a person has, because all involve irrational fear and dread, and symptoms are often similar. "

For many who suffer from PTSD, extreme fear is also a way of life be-cause whatever horror they expe-rienced continues to haunt them. Symptoms usually develop within a few months of the traumatic incident. In some cases, though, years go by before any sign of PTSD is evident, and then something triggers a memory of what happened. These flashbacks cause people to relive the traumatic occurrence in their thoughts during the daytime and in night-mares when they sleep. As the NIMH explains: "Flashbacks may consist of images, sounds, smells, or feelings, and are often triggered by ordinary occurrences, such as a door slamming or a car backfiring on the street. A person having a flashback may lose touch with reality and believe that the traumatic incident is happening all over again."[16]

Two U.S. soldiers take cover during a gun battle in Iraq. Exposure to combat is a leading cause of post-traumatic stress disorder, or PTSD. This anxiety disorder causes a person to experience intense fear, anger, and helplessness.

Phobias are not the same as PTSD, but they can also significantly interfere with one's life. This has been Grossman's experience, because his phobia often flares up without warning. He writes:

> It doesn't take much to set mine off. A swig from a water bottle can do it, or someone chewing gum. Every morning when I get on the subway, I scan the passengers like an air marshal looking for terrorists. At any moment, somebody could whip out a bagel or a danish. I do well in restaurants, where there's a lot of ambient noise and distraction, but one-on-one meals are a minefield. And don't get me started on popcorn. When I go to a movie theater, every movie is a horror movie.[17]

How Anxiety Disorders Are Diagnosed

Unlike many diseases, there is no laboratory test that can diagnose anxiety disorders. As health journalist Irene Wielawski writes: "Psychiatric illness is not as easily diagnosed as, say, an infection, where a simple blood test can yield definitive answers. For anxiety disorders, it is important to assess the degree of anxiety in specific situations to determine whether it is interfering with work, school, personal relationships or other aspects of daily life."[18] If a patient exhibits symptoms of extreme anxiety, a physician will do a complete medical history and perform an examination to determine whether a physical illness is at the root of the problem. If all other potential reasons for the patient's symptoms have been ruled out, he or she will likely be referred to a psychotherapist, a professional who is trained in diagnosing mental illnesses.

Through a series of psychological interviews and assessments, the therapist evaluates whether the patient suffers from one or more anxiety disorders. This can be challenging, however, even for the most experienced professionals, because anxiety disorder symptoms are often similar to those of other mental illnesses such as depression, bipolar disorder, and schizophrenia. Also, it can be difficult to determine which anxiety disorder or disorders a person has, because all involve irrational fear and dread, and symptoms are often similar.

> **Conquering anxiety disorders can be a painful, seemingly impossible task for many who suffer from them.**

Treating Anxiety Disorders

The treatment that is recommended for people with anxiety disorders varies based on the patient and how severe his or her disorder is. Typically, treatment consists of a combination of medications and a type of psychotherapy known as cognitive behavioral therapy, or CBT. By undergoing CBT, patients learn to face their fears head-on and challenge their irrational thoughts. The hope is that they can change the thinking patterns that lead to feelings of fear and anxiety, thus "rewiring" their brains. As psychologist Patrick B. McGrath writes: "A basic facet of CBT is that therapists can use three things to understand their patients—the way people think, feel, and behave. Further, the goal of this therapy is to help people make changes in their behaviors, thoughts, and feelings."[19]

In an effort to conquer his phobia of being around people who eat and drink, Grossman has participated in CBT treatment. In some sessions he took groceries with him and watched as his psychiatrist ate the food. He writes:

> I would calmly try to separate the sight and sound of a person eating from the fear it induced in me. I would try to retrain my brain to be unafraid of something that there was no reason to be afraid of in the first place. . . . As the treatment went on, I began to catch my first glimpses of what it might be like to live without wanting to cross the street every time I saw a stranger holding an ice cream cone.[20]

Can People Overcome Anxiety Disorders?

Conquering anxiety disorders can be a painful, seemingly impossible task for many who suffer from them. A major reason why so many cannot get well is that they do not seek professional help. According to the Anxiety Disorders Association of America, only about one-third of people suffering from one or more anxiety disorders receive treatment, often because they are ashamed of their irrational fears. Yet even with treatment, anxiety disorders can be extremely difficult to overcome, as Grossman knows from experience. Although he has worked very hard to overcome his phobia, his treatment has not been successful. "Maybe that means there's more to the problem than bad wiring," he writes. "There are feelings down there too—old, dark, unmapped feelings— and I'm going to have to deal with them before the fear leaves me alone. My phobia is a part of me—an ugly part, by the looks of it. I'm going to have to get to know that demon better. Because it's not going to leave till it's good and ready."[21]

Although not everyone with anxiety disorders can overcome them, numerous sufferers can and do recover. Panic disorder, for instance, is considered to be one of the most treatable anxiety disorders, with a success rate of up to 90 percent for those who seek treatment. Other anxiety disorders can be overcome as well, as the NIMH explains: "Effective therapies for anxiety disorders are available, and research is uncovering new treatments that can help most people with anxiety disorders lead productive, fulfilling lives."[22]

A Perplexing Mental Health Issue

Anxiety disorders are diverse, complex, and often misunderstood. Research has revealed clues about these disorders, and treatments have vastly improved people's chances of having a better quality of life. As studies continue, this may result in fewer people being plagued by the intense, irrational fear that is the hallmark of anxiety disorders—and is a constant source of misery for those who suffer from them.

What Are Anxiety Disorders?

> ❝Most people feel anxious about something for a short time now and again, but people with anxiety disorders feel this way most of the time. Their fears and worries make it hard for them to do everyday tasks.❞

—National Institute of Mental Health, which seeks to reduce mental illness and behavioral disorders through research.

> ❝Unlike the relatively mild, brief anxiety caused by a stressful event such as a business presentation or a first date, anxiety disorders are chronic, relentless, and can grow progressively worse if not treated.❞

—Grace Tsai, a psychologist who writes about a variety of mental health issues.

Throughout history noted physicians have observed and written about patients who suffered from intense fears and dread for which there was no apparent explanation. Such fears would likely be categorized as anxiety disorders today, but centuries ago even the most learned scholars were mystified by them. Yet they were also intrigued by these strange fears, which became known as phobias. The word has roots in Greek mythology, named after Phobos, the god who personified fear and incited terror and panic, especially among the enemies of those who chose to worship him.

Phobias were a topic of particular interest during the eighteenth century. In 1798 American physician Benjamin Rush published an essay entitled "On the Different Species of Phobia," in which he defined phobias as "a fear of an imaginary evil, or an undue fear of a real one."[23]

Rush listed numerous phobias that he had observed, including the fear of cats. He wrote about his personal observations of "several gentlemen of unquestionable courage, who have retreated a thousand times from the sight of a cat; and who have even discovered signs of fear and terror upon being confined in a room with a cat that was out of sight."[24] When he observed rat phobia, Rush attributed the fear primarily to women: "It is peculiar, in some measure, to the female sex. I know several ladies who never fail to discover their terror by screaming at the sight of a rat; and who cannot even sleep within the noise of that animal."[25]

Fight or Flight Gone Awry

Anxiety is a normal part of being human and is a by-product of people's natural response to danger. If they are faced with a threatening situation or perceive that one exists, they instinctively question whether they should stay and fight or run away. This phenomenon, known as the fight-or-flight response, is activated by the adrenal glands. These two glands, that sit atop the kidneys, secrete bursts of stress hormones such as cortisol and adrenaline. As these chemicals course through the bloodstream, the heart rate speeds up, senses sharpen, and people become more alert and focused. This prepares them to take whatever action is necessary to deal with (or escape from) dangerous or threatening circumstances.

> " The natural fight-or-flight response is often said to have somehow gone haywire in people with anxiety disorders. "

The natural fight-or-flight response is often said to have somehow gone haywire in people with anxiety disorders. Their anxiety surfaces not only when an actual threatening situation arises, but all the time, even when no threat or danger exists. As the mental health Web site HealthyPlace explains:

> Unfortunately, when the fear or anxiety is internal, there is nothing external to fight. There is nowhere to run. We are caught with the internal physical response. These symptoms are sensitive to the "what ifs"—fearful thinking that accompanies Anxiety Disorders. With every

fearful thought, the fight-or-flight response is triggered, adrenalin released, and physical symptoms occur."[26]

A vicious cycle results in which fearful thoughts increase, more adrenaline is released, and symptoms build.

Anxiety in Overdrive

The term *social anxiety* could apply to any number of uncomfortable social situations, from being nervous before giving a speech in a high school class to being self-conscious about attending a dance or football game without a friend along. But social anxiety disorder (or social phobia) goes much deeper than that, as the NIMH explains:

> People with social phobia have an intense, persistent, and chronic fear of being watched and judged by others and of doing things that will embarrass them. They can worry for days or weeks before a dreaded situation. . . . Even if they manage to confront their fears and be around others, they are usually very anxious beforehand, are intensely uncomfortable throughout the encounter, and worry about how they were judged for hours afterward.[27]

A Naperville, Illinois, woman named Gail posted a comment on a public radio program site about her painful struggle with social anxiety disorder. She was shy as a young girl but had no problem making friends, did well in school, and was comfortable speaking in public. As the years went by, this began to change, and Gail became increasingly anxious in social situations. This worried her, but everyone insisted that the anxiety was nothing more than a sign of her shyness. She explains:

> I'd hear it over and over again how "everyone" is shy. "Everyone" has problems talking to new people. I honestly thought that I must be a very weak willed person to not be able to get over feeling like I was going to die if I had to walk up to that unknown person at a party. I thought "everyone" hyperventilated at the idea of talking to a professor. I thought "everyone" was completely unable to answer their phone at home. Honestly, I thought everyone felt that way, and everyone but me just got over it.[28]

Gail's fear of social situations continued to worsen until there was no doubt in her mind that her problem could not be blamed on ordinary shyness. By the time she was diagnosed with social anxiety disorder, she was nearing the point of being totally incapacitated by her fears. "I could barely drag myself to work," she writes. "I could not talk to strangers at all, and I had no friends. I had one long suffering boyfriend who had to deal with my locking myself in the bathroom and crying when he tried to have me talk to his aunt on the phone." Once doctors were finally able to give Gail a name for her disorder, her life began to change for the better. "It was like a light bulb going off," she says. "It was the first time that I realized that it wasn't normal to feel the way I felt."[29]

Unfathomable Fear

Because people with social anxiety disorder are fearful of most any type of social situation, life can be enormously difficult—but for those who suffer from agoraphobia, this sense of fear and dread is far more intense. People with agoraphobia cannot tolerate being away from a safe place, appearing in public, or being in any situation from which they feel there is no escape. Eventually they reach the point of seeking refuge inside their homes and stop going anywhere at all, as psychiatrist David L. Ginsberg writes: "People with agoraphobia often avoid being out alone, going to supermarkets, traveling in trains or airplanes, crossing bridges, climbing to heights, going through tunnels, crossing open fields, and riding in elevators."[30]

> " Because people with social anxiety disorder are fearful of most any type of social situation, life can be enormously difficult—but for those who suffer from agoraphobia, this sense of fear and dread is far more intense. "

Fiona Bradshaw knows from personal experience how terrifying agoraphobia can be. Although she does not recall when she was first stricken with it, the disorder has caused her to become completely housebound, "tethered to home." She writes: "I have, for all intents and purposes, become a prisoner in my own life."

Bradshaw talks freely about the unbearable pain that agoraphobia has caused her: "My disability, my crippling ailment, is invisible and I'm certainly not guaranteed to die from it although sometimes I wouldn't mind slipping away from the constant fear. I can't see my agoraphobia and panic attacks but I can feel them when they course through my body."[31]

The Curse of Phobias

Like other anxiety disorders, phobias are often compared with the normal stress and anxious feelings that all humans experience from time to time—but that perception is flawed. While it is true that most everyone is afraid of *something*, people with phobias are plagued by inexplicable, morbid fears of objects, situations, and/or places. As the book *The A to Z of Phobias, Fears, and Anxieties* explains: "The primary difference between a normal fear that is shared by many people and a chronic phobia is that a phobia is irrational and impedes the individual's daily life. When the fear becomes overwhelming, persistent, and enveloping and impedes an individual from normal functioning, it is considered a phobia."[32]

The authors illustrate the difference between normal fears and phobias by acknowledging that many people do not like snakes or spiders and may even fear them to some extent. But their emotions do not involve the same all-encompassing terror as phobias, whereby sufferers have "irrationally excessive fears and may exhibit a marked reaction to even a drawing or the mere *thought* of snakes and spiders (or another feared object)."[33]

> Like other anxiety disorders, phobias are often compared with the normal stress and anxious feelings that all humans experience from time to time—but that perception is flawed.

People who suffer from phobias may manage to live somewhat normally as long as they can avoid the situations or objects that they fear. But if such avoidance is not possible, the disorder can overtake one's life. One person who suffers from numerous phobias is American music composer Allen Shawn, who shares his experiences: "I don't like heights. I don't like being on the water. I am upset by walking across parking lots or open parks or fields where there are no buildings. I tend to avoid bridges, unless they are on a small scale." Shawn says that he is severely claustrophobic, and he describes how this causes him to avoid any situation where he could potentially feel closed-in: "When I go to a theater, I sit on the aisle. I am petrified of tunnels, making most train travel as well as many drives difficult. I don't take subways. I avoid elevators as much as possible. I experience glassed-in spaces as toxic, and I find it very difficult to adjust to being in buildings in which the windows don't open."[34]

When Obsessions Crowd Out Reason

Many people refer to themselves as "neat freaks" because they cannot stand a cluttered home, a messy desk, pictures hanging crookedly on the wall, or any sort of disorganization. If they are teased about this penchant for perfectionism, they may quip, "Oh it's just my OCD kicking in." But the fact is, real obsessive-compulsive disorder is no joking matter. Those who suffer from its most severe forms go far, far beyond the need for order, neatness, and organization—they are haunted by obsessive thoughts to the point that they feel life is no longer within their control.

An article in the July–August 2008 issue of *Men's Health* offered an example of the difference between being detail oriented and having OCD. A man drives to his office building, parks his car, gets out, and starts to head inside. Then it suddenly occurs to him that he may have forgotten to lock the car, so he goes back to check, sees that the car is locked, and does not worry about it anymore. This same scenario would be very, very different for a person with OCD, as psychologist Jeff Szymanski explains: "Someone with OCD says, 'I went and checked the car, but did I really check it? I'm looking at my hand turning the key in the lock, but is that perception really clear enough? Did I hear the click, or do I just remember hearing the click, or did I hear the click last time I checked this?"[35]

Many people with OCD are convinced that if they do not perform certain rituals, their inaction will bring harm to their loved ones or even to strangers. This was the case with radio broadcaster Jeff Bell, who lived in fear that he would inadvertently harm someone. This became a serious problem whenever Bell was driving his car, because whenever he hit a pothole or a small bump in the road, he found it impossible just to drive

> **Many people with OCD are convinced that if they do not perform certain rituals, their inaction will bring harm to their loved ones or even to strangers.**

away. Instead, he had to turn the car around and go back to make sure that he had not run over somebody—even though he knew that his fear was irrational and probably unfounded.

In an attempt to avoid these imagined hazards, Bell started walking to and from work, but that presented a whole new set of challenges. If he saw a twig lying on the sidewalk, his initial thought was to move it so no one would trip over it. But what if even moving it slightly created a hazard for a bicyclist? He then considered moving the twig to a different location, but doing that might cause a worse problem—someone might get hurt who would not have been injured if he had just left it alone. Bell agonized over this, going back and forth and fretting about what he should do. Finally, he picked the twig up and carried it with him "rather than leave it anywhere it could potentially be a problem."[36]

A Painful Way to Live

Whether people suffer from phobias, an extreme dread of social situations, or haunting obsessions, their lives revolve around fear and uncertainty. They are often misunderstood by friends and family, some of whom may think they are extremely shy or even just prone to overreaction. But anxiety disorders are not about shyness or overreacting. As Cathy Frank, director of Outpatient Behavioral Health Services at Detroit's Henry Ford Hospital, notes, anxiety disorders are "a chronic illness that has a significant impact on your daily function and may rob you of any joy in your life."[37]

Primary Source Quotes*

What Are Anxiety Disorders?

" Almost everyone feels anxious at times. Anxiety is a common experience, particularly as a response to life stresses. However, severe and uncontrollable anxiety can become a disabling condition. "

—David L. Ginsberg, foreword to *100 Questions and Answers About Panic Disorder*, by Carol W. Berman. Sudbury, MA: Jones and Bartlett, 2010.

Ginsberg is a clinical associate professor in the department of psychiatry at New York University School of Medicine.

" Most phobics know that their extreme fears are irrational and may even seem silly, yet they continue to be transfixed by them, trapped and unable to escape from them. "

—Ronald M. Doctor, Ada P. Kahn, and Christine Adamec, *The A to Z of Phobias, Fears, and Anxieties*. New York: Checkmark, 2008.

Doctor is a psychology professor at California State University, and Kahn and Adamec are authors who specialize in health and medical issues.

* Editor's Note: While the definition of a primary source can be narrowly or broadly defined, for the purposes of Compact Research, a primary source consists of: 1) results of original research presented by an organization or researcher; 2) eyewitness accounts of events, personal experience, or work experience; 3) first-person editorials offering pundits' opinions; 4) government officials presenting political plans and/or policies; 5) representatives of organizations presenting testimony or policy.

> **"Anxiety disorders are one of the most common psychiatric disorders in children and adolescents, but they often go undetected or untreated."**

—Sucheta D. Connolly and Sonali D. Nanayakkara, "Anxiety Disorders in Children and Adolescents," *Psychiatric Times*, October 8, 2009. www.psychiatrictimes.com.

Connolly and Nanayakkara are psychiatry professors at the University of Illinois–Chicago.

> **"Social anxiety disorder (SAD), also referred to as social phobia, is a chronic and potentially disabling anxiety disorder characterized by the intense and persistent fear of being scrutinized or negatively evaluated by others."**

—Sy Atezaz Saeed, "Social Anxiety Disorder: An Update on Evidence-Based Treatment Options," *Psychiatric Times*, May 2009. www.cmellc.com.

Saeed is a professor and chair of the Department of Psychiatric Medicine at the Brody School of Medicine at East Carolina University and chief of psychiatry at Pitt Memorial Hospital in Greenville, North Carolina.

> **"Agoraphobics are afraid of being outside their homes alone, being in a crowd, standing in a line, being on a bridge, or of traveling in a bus, train or car."**

—Carol W. Berman, *100 Questions and Answers About Panic Disorder*. Sudbury, MA: Jones and Bartlett, 2010.

Berman is a clinical instructor of psychiatry at New York University Medical School.

> **"General Anxiety Disorder is the big anxiety disorder that people tend to miss. With the others—Post Traumatic Stress Disorder, separation anxiety, and social phobia—it's more obvious when you have it."**

—Edge Foundation, "The 4 Most Common Anxiety Disorders Associated with ADHD: Anxiety and ADHD—part 2," February 2009. www.edgefoundation.org.

The Edge Foundation's mission is to help all children and adults with attention-deficit/hyperactivity disorder fulfill their own potential, personal vision, and passion.

66 One of the most frightening anxiety disorders is panic disorder. 99

—Robert L. Leahy, "Do You Have Panic Disorder?" *Psychology Today*, April 10, 2009. www.psychologytoday.com.

Leahy is a clinical professor of psychology at Weill-Cornell Medical School, as well as director of the American Institute for Cognitive Therapy.

66 In social anxiety disorder, everyday interactions cause extreme fear and self-consciousness. It may become impossible for you to eat with acquaintances or write a check in public, let alone go to a party with lots of strangers. 99

—Mayo Clinic, "Social Anxiety Disorder (Social Phobia)," August 28, 2009. www.mayoclinic.com.

The Mayo Clinic is a world-renowned medical facility headquartered in Rochester, Minnesota.

66 Not every episode of panic indicates a full blown panic disorder. When a person experiences repeated episodes of panic resulting in heightened anxiety that may be debilitating, then the diagnosis of panic disorder is considered. 99

—Clare Steffen, "5 Things You Need to Know About Panic Disorder in Teens," LiveStrong, November 8, 2009. www.livestrong.com.

Steffen is a psychologist who offers marriage, family, and child/adolescent therapy.

What Are Anxiety Disorders?

- According to the Anxiety Disorders Association of America, anxiety disorders collectively represent the most common mental illness in the United States, affecting **40 million** adults in the United States aged 18 and older (which is 18 percent of the population).

- The National Institute of Mental Health states that an estimated **2.2 million** Americans suffer from obsessive-compulsive disorder, and the disease affects men and women equally.

- According to psychiatrist Sy Atezaz Saeed, **social anxiety disorder** is the third most common psychiatric disorder in the United States after depression and substance abuse.

- The Anxiety Disorders Foundation states that generalized anxiety disorder affects as much as **5 percent** of the U.S. population and tends to be more common in women than in men.

- The National Institute of Mental Health states that panic disorder affects **6 million** people in the United States and is twice as common among women as among men.

- According to the Anxiety Disorders Association of America, anxiety disorders affect **one in eight children**.

- The American Psychological Association states that **10 percent to 25 percent** of the U.S. population suffers from aviophobia, which is a fear of flying.

Anxiety Is the Most Common Mental Health Problem

Of all the major mental health disorders that affect people in the United States, anxiety disorders collectively represent the most common, as this graph illustrates.

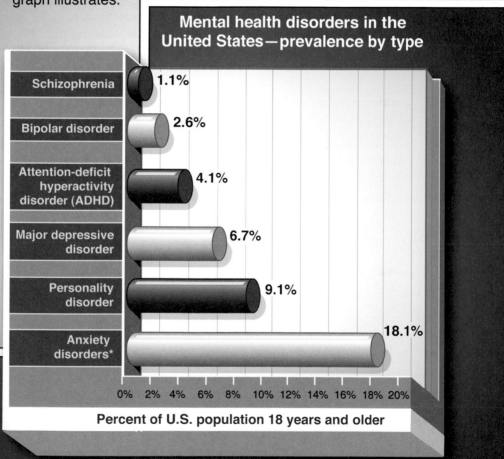

Mental health disorders in the United States—prevalence by type

Schizophrenia	1.1%
Bipolar disorder	2.6%
Attention-deficit hyperactivity disorder (ADHD)	4.1%
Major depressive disorder	6.7%
Personality disorder	9.1%
Anxiety disorders*	18.1%

0% 2% 4% 6% 8% 10% 12% 14% 16% 18% 20%

Percent of U.S. population 18 years and older

* Included in anxiety disorders are panic disorder, obsessive-compulsive disorder, post-traumatic stress disorder, generalized anxiety disorder, social phobia, and specific phobia.

Source: National Institute of Mental Health, "The Numbers Count: Mental Disorders in America," July 21, 2010. www.nimh.nih.gov.

Phobias

Most everyone experiences fear from time to time, but those with phobias live with extreme fear and dread that goes far beyond what is considered normal. This diagram shows some examples of phobias, some of which are common while others are far less prevalent.

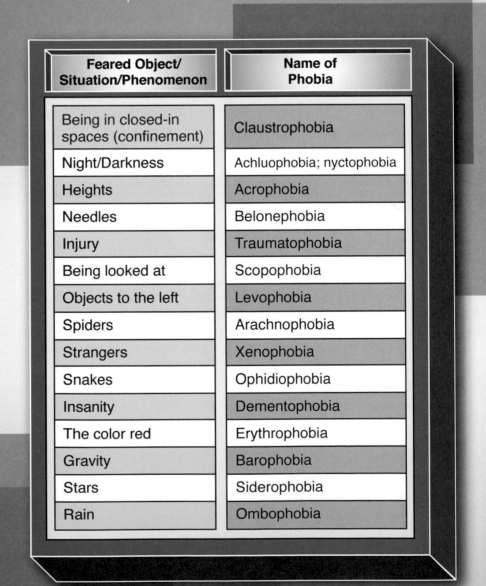

Feared Object/ Situation/Phenomenon	Name of Phobia
Being in closed-in spaces (confinement)	Claustrophobia
Night/Darkness	Achluophobia; nyctophobia
Heights	Acrophobia
Needles	Belonephobia
Injury	Traumatophobia
Being looked at	Scopophobia
Objects to the left	Levophobia
Spiders	Arachnophobia
Strangers	Xenophobia
Snakes	Ophidiophobia
Insanity	Dementophobia
The color red	Erythrophobia
Gravity	Barophobia
Stars	Siderophobia
Rain	Ombophobia

Source: Ronald M. Doctor, Ada P. Kahn, and Christine Adamec, *The A to Z of Phobias, Fears, and Anxieties.* New York: Checkmark, 2008, p. xvii.

All Ages Are Vulnerable

Anxiety disorders affect people of all ages and, according to the National Institute of Mental Health, can strike at any time from childhood to adulthood. This graph illustrates the mean age of onset for the various types of anxiety disorders.

Anxiety Disorders—Mean age of onset

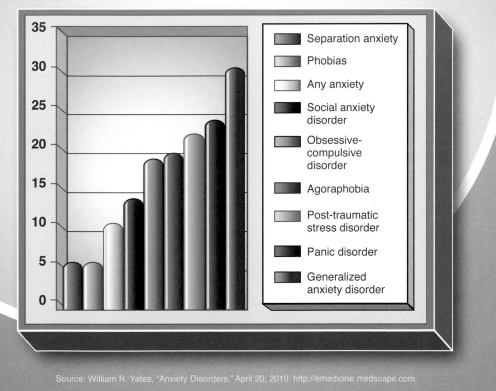

Source: William R. Yates, "Anxiety Disorders," April 20, 2010. http://emedicine.medscape.com.

- The Edge Foundation states that an estimated **50 percent** of adults with attention-deficit/hyperactivity disorder will also suffer from generalized anxiety disorder during their lifetimes, compared with **5 percent** of adults in the general population.

- According to the Anxiety Disorders Foundation, panic disorder combined with agoraphobia affects roughly **5 percent** of the U.S. population.

- OCD Chicago, an OCD information Web site, states that an estimated **40 percent** of people with the eating disorder anorexia nervosa also suffer from obsessive-compulsive disorder.

- According to the University of Maryland Medical Center, each year up to **9 percent** of Americans experience one or more phobias that range from mild to severe.

- The National Anxiety Foundation states that panic disorder begins most often between **20 and 30 years of age**.

What Causes
Anxiety Disorders?

❝It is believed that a combination of biological factors, brain functions, personal circumstances, combined with social and economic factors, cause anxiety disorders, the same way that heart disease or diabetes are caused by a combination of factors.❞

—Health Canada, the Canadian government's principal public health agency.

❝As with many mental health conditions, what causes generalized anxiety disorder isn't fully understood. . . . It's likely that the condition has several causes that may include genetics, your environment and stress.❞

—Mayo Clinic, a world-renowned medical facility headquartered in Rochester, Minnesota.

For anyone who suffers from an anxiety disorder, being told that the cause is unknown can be extremely frustrating—yet that is what people usually hear. Unlike many diseases for which medical science has revealed a definitive cause or causes, such is not the case with anxiety disorders. Scientists have many theories, and research has produced promising findings, but there are still more questions than answers. The Mayo Clinic explains: "As with many mental health conditions, the exact cause of anxiety disorders isn't fully understood. It's thought that anxiety disorders may involve an imbalance of naturally occurring brain chemicals. . . . Life experiences such as traumatic events appear to trigger anxiety disorders in people who are already prone to becoming anxious. Inherited traits also are a factor."[38]

This description refers to the complex interaction of genetics, brain chemistry, and environmental factors, all of which are believed to work together in the development of anxiety disorders. This theory is widely accepted by mental health professionals, which is why an analogy is often used when referring to the cause: Biology may load the gun, but the environment pulls the trigger.

The Importance of Brain Chemistry

Even with all the uncertainty about the cause of anxiety disorders, it is widely accepted among scientists that the brain plays a pivotal role. The most complicated organ in the human body, the brain is responsible for intelligence, memories, thoughts, imagination, feelings, behavior, and body movement. The key to the brain's functioning is its complex network of cells, known as neurons, which rapidly fire messages to each other and to various parts of the body in the form of electrical signals. This constant communication is made possible by chemical messengers known as neurotransmitters, which transfer the signals from one neuron to another.

Scientists have identified four neurotransmitters that they believe are related to anxiety disorders. These include serotonin, a brain chemical that helps regulate emotions, feelings, and mood; and dopamine, which is also connected to emotions and feelings of pleasure. The other two neurotransmitters are epinephrine, which is associated with feelings of alertness, fear, anxiety, and panic, and gamma-aminobutyric acid (GABA), which helps to regulate the brain's excitation mechanism by preventing neurons from over-firing. As anxiety disorders specialist Sheryl Ankrom writes: "For optimal brain function, neurotransmitters must be carefully balanced and orchestrated. They are often interconnected and rely on each other for proper function. For example, the neurotransmitter GABA, which induces relaxation, can only function properly with adequate amounts of serotonin."[39]

Even with all the uncertainty about the cause of anxiety disorders, it is widely accepted among scientists that the brain plays a pivotal role.

Serotonin has long been implicated in the development of anxiety disorders, since insufficient levels can interfere with the brain's normal function and behavior. Many scientists are convinced that the chemical plays a key role in anxiety disorders because they have seen how medications known as selective serotonin reuptake inhibitors (SSRIs) bring serotonin levels back to normal. As the Anxiety Disorders Association of America explains: "SSRIs relieve symptoms by blocking the reabsorption, or reuptake, of serotonin by certain nerve cells in the brain. This leaves more serotonin available, which improves mood."[40]

Brain Imaging Revelations

Scientists have long suspected that brain chemistry contributes to the development of anxiety disorders. In the May 2008 issue of the *Journal of Nuclear Medicine*, researchers from the Netherlands announced the results of a study confirming a common biological condition among those who suffer from social anxiety disorder. The study involved 12 people who had been diagnosed with the disorder but were not taking any medications to treat it, and a control group of 12 healthy participants.

To perform the study, the team used a type of test that shows how blood flows to tissues and organs. First both groups were injected with a compound that binds with elements of the brain's serotonin and dopamine systems. Then the researchers took measurements in the areas of the brain that are known to be influenced by those chemicals.

By observing the brains of the patients with social anxiety disorder, the researchers could detect distinct irregularities in the dopamine and serotonin neurotransmitters. Nic J.A. van der Wee, a psychiatrist who specializes in anxiety disorders and the study's lead researcher, explains the significance of this finding: "We found the first direct evidence for abnormalities of the brain's dopaminergic system in patients with social anxiety disorder. The study demonstrates that social anxiety has a physical brain-dependent component."[41]

Secrets Within Genes

The genetic component of anxiety disorders has been of interest to scientists for years. Because a number of these disorders exist and each has its own complex patterns of inheritance, identifying specific genes has been challenging. Research has shown, however, that some, if not all, of the disorders are hereditary. For example, studies performed with twins have clearly indicated that social anxiety disorder runs in families. If someone has the disorder, the risk of an immediate family member developing it is about 10 times higher than for the general population. Obsessive-compulsive disorder has also been shown to have a strong hereditary component: An estimated 25 percent of people who suffer from OCD have an immediate family member who also has it. The rate is significantly higher among twins. If one identical twin has OCD, the other has a 70 percent change of also developing it. With fraternal twins, the risk is about 50 percent.

> Studies performed with twins have clearly indicated that social anxiety disorder runs in families, with the risk for immediate family members suffering from the disorder being about 10 times higher than for the general population.

Previous studies performed with mice have associated an area of chromosome 1 (the largest human chromosome) with anxious temperament. Particular focus has been on the gene responsible for making RGS2, a protein that plays an important role in anxiety and/or aggressiveness by mediating the activity of neurotransmitter receptors. When scientists "knocked out" the RGS2 gene in the mice (meaning they rendered it inoperative), the creatures' behavior grew increasingly fearful, which suggested a strong association between RGS2 and anxiety disorders.

Convincing Genetic Findings

A study published in the March 2008 issue of *Archives of General Psychiatry* expanded on prior RGS2 research—and provided some of the strongest evidence to date that genetic factors are closely associated with anxiety disorders. To examine more comprehensively the connection between RGS2 and anxiety disorders, researchers from Massachusetts General Hospital, the University of California–San Diego, and Yale University conducted a two-part study with human subjects. The first part involved analyzing blood samples from children to evaluate their levels of behavioral inhibition. This refers to temperament traits such as withdrawal, avoidance, and fear of the unfamiliar, which are linked to increased risk of anxiety disorders. By testing several sites in the RGS2 gene, researchers identified 9 variations that appeared to be associated with inhibition.

The second part of the study involved more than 700 college students who had completed questionnaires designed to measure their personality traits. The researchers analyzed blood samples from the participants, looking for the four genetic markers that had demonstrated the strongest effects in the children involved in the first experiment. The team found that the markers associated with inhibited behavior in the children were also common in the college students who scored high on measures of introversion (another personality trait that involves social inhibition) on their questionnaires.

> **People with anxiety disorders are the first to say that the emotional pain they suffer from day to day is every bit as bad as physical pain—and in 2009 researchers from the University of California–Los Angeles discovered a biological basis for this.**

Together, these experiments showed that certain versions of the RGS2 gene were more common in both children and adults who were assessed as being inhibited or introverted. These versions of the gene were also associated with increased activity of brain regions involved in emotional processing. Jordan Smoller, the study's lead researcher, explains why this is an important finding: "We found that variations in this gene were associated with shy, inhibited behavior in children, introverted personality in adults, and the reactivity of brain regions involved in processing fear and anxiety. Each of these traits appears to be a risk factor for social anxiety disorder, the most common type of anxiety disorder in the U.S."[42]

The Pain Gene

People with anxiety disorders are the first to say that the emotional pain they suffer from day to day is every bit as bad as physical pain—and in

2009 researchers from the University of California–Los Angeles discovered a biological basis for this. Past studies have shown that a gene called OPRM1 regulates opioids, the brain's natural painkillers. Variations in this gene can lead to a more intense sensation of pain in someone who has a physical injury. Based on the new study, the same gene variation also appears to regulate levels of emotional distress when people experience hurt feelings due to social situations.

The researchers performed magnetic resonance imaging (MRI) scans of the brains of participants while at the same time exposing them to a computer program that simulated social rejection. Those with a variation in the OPRM1 gene reported higher levels of distress in response to social rejection. At the same time they were having the emotional reaction, the scans showed heightened activity in the regions of the brain that are associated with social pain. As a result of the study, activity in these pain-related regions has been definitively connected to the OPRM1 gene.

> **Of all the anxiety disorders, none is more closely connected to environmental factors than post-traumatic stress disorder.**

In a 2009 post on the OCD Center of Los Angeles blog, Stacey Kuhl-Wochner, a clinical social worker with the treatment center, says that this finding provides "some of the most advanced clues yet as to why some people experience social rejection with such force." She adds, "And for those with social anxiety disorder, these studies not only provide evidence that their suffering is real, but also provide hopeful avenues for future research that may one day lead to better treatments for this condition."[43]

Trauma Triggers

Of all the anxiety disorders, none is more closely connected to environmental factors than post-traumatic stress disorder. PTSD strikes people who have lived through an experience that was so horrifying and traumatic that the memories haunt them to the point of incapacitation. Yet as strong as the environmental component of PTSD is, scientists have long speculated that biological factors may also be involved. Cathy Frank says that some anxiety can be caused solely by environmental stressors. "But," she adds, "we don't yet know why two people could experience similar stress such as a trauma, an assault, and have very different reactions. One may deal with it normally, one may develop posttraumatic stress disorder."[44]

The potential connection between biological factors and PTSD was the subject of an extensive study published in the December 2008 issue of *Psychiatric Genetics*. A team of researchers from the University of California–Los Angeles tracked people from 12 multigenerational families who had survived a catastrophic earthquake that struck northern Armenia in December 1988. The quake destroyed 58 towns and villages, killed at least 25,000 people, injured 19,000 others, and left 500,000 people homeless. To analyze the effects of the natural disaster on the study's participants, the researchers obtained detailed information about their personal experiences during the quake, including destruction of residences, deaths of relatives, seeing dead bodies, sustaining injuries, and/or witnessing the injuries of others. The participants were also asked questions about their fears of the earthquake itself: of getting hurt, of dying, and of whether they feared that someone else would be badly hurt or killed. In addition, the team assessed the participants' symptoms of PTSD, anxiety, and chronic depression.

By analyzing the wealth of information that was collected during the study, the team found that 41 percent of PTSD symptoms and 66 percent of anxiety symptoms in participants were attributable to genetic factors. Principal researcher Amen Goenjian explains why this project was unique, as well as extremely valuable: "This was a study of multigenerational family members—parents and offspring, grandparents and grandchildren, siblings, and so on—and we found that the genetic makeup of some of these individuals renders them more vulnerable to develop PTSD, anxiety, and depressive symptoms."[45]

Lingering Mysteries

Scientists have been searching for answers about the cause of anxiety disorders for years, and a great deal of progress has been made. Studies have revealed crucial information about the role of brain chemistry, genetics, and the environment, and how these factors work together in the development of anxiety disorders. Many unanswered questions remain, however, and scientists are hopeful that future research will provide answers.

What Causes Anxiety Disorders?

Primary Source Quotes

66 Some experts believe that phobias are hardwired into the brain as evolutional rudiments (called *prepared fears*), while others believe they stem from unresolved conflicts in childhood or traumas. 99

—Ronald M. Doctor, Ada P. Kahn, and Christine Adamec, *The A to Z of Phobias, Fears, and Anxieties*. New York: Checkmark, 2008.

Doctor is a psychology professor at California State University, and Kahn and Adamec are authors who specialize in health and medical issues.

66 Most scientists now believe that anxiety disorders involve hyperactivity in a channel of the central nervous system called the fear network. 99

—Jack M. Gorman, "Anxiety and Panic—the Dana Guide," Dana Foundation, June 2009. www.dana.org.

Gorman is a professor and vice-chair for research in the Department of Psychiatry at Columbia University in New York City.

* Editor's Note: While the definition of a primary source can be narrowly or broadly defined, for the purposes of Compact Research, a primary source consists of: 1) results of original research presented by an organization or researcher; 2) eyewitness accounts of events, personal experience, or work experience; 3) first-person editorials offering pundits' opinions; 4) government officials presenting political plans and/or policies; 5) representatives of organizations presenting testimony or policy.

66 **One theory has it that panic attacks are caused by a falsely activated alarm system in the brain.** 99

—Carol W. Berman, *100 Questions and Answers About Panic Disorder*. Sudbury, MA: Jones and Bartlett, 2010.

Berman is a clinical instructor of psychiatry at New York University Medical School.

66 **Panic disorder sometimes runs in families, but no one knows for sure why some people have it, while others don't. When chemicals in the brain are not at a certain level it can cause a person to have panic disorder.** 99

—National Institute of Mental Health, *When Fear Overwhelms: Panic Disorder*, 2008. www.nimh.nih.gov.

The National Institute of Mental Health seeks to reduce mental illness and behavioral disorders through basic and clinical research.

66 **Researchers believe that the relationship between anxiety disorders and long-term exposure to abuse, violence, or poverty is an important area for further study, as life experiences may affect an individual's susceptibility to these disorders.** 99

—University of Maryland Medical Center, "Anxiety Disorders—Causes," February 5, 2008. www.umm.edu.

A teaching hospital located in Baltimore, the University of Maryland Medical Center provides a full range of health care to people throughout Maryland and the mid-Atlantic region.

66 **Childhood factors also can contribute. If your parents were overprotective, you may lack confidence and perceive the world as dangerous. If your parents were critical, you may struggle with social anxiety.** 99

—Pamela Wampler, "Path to Peace," *St. Louis Woman*, April 2009. www.stlouiswomanmag.com.

Wampler is a licensed psychotherapist who suffers from severe panic attacks.

66 It is important to note that although a few experts say it is more common in persons who experienced a separation experience as a child, many of experts feel that Panic Disorder afflicts emotionally healthy people. 99

—National Anxiety Foundation, "Panic Disorder," 2010. www.lexington-on-line.com.

The National Anxiety Foundation is an organization that seeks to educate the public about anxiety through printed and electronic media.

66 The cause of PDA [panic disorder with agoraphobia] is unknown. There are biological and psychological theories that have been supported by research. 99

—Anxiety Disorders Foundation, "Anxiety Disorders," 2009. www.anxietydisordersfoundation.org.

The Anxiety Disorders Foundation seeks to improve the lives of everyone who is affected by anxiety disorders.

66 Many cognitive theorists believe that people with OCD have faulty or dysfunctional beliefs, and that it's how they misinterpret their intrusive thoughts that lead to obsessions and compulsions. 99

—OCD Chicago, "What Causes OCD?" 2010. www.ocdchicago.org.

OCD Chicago seeks to increase awareness of obsessive-compulsive disorder, as well as encourage research into new treatments and a cure.

Facts and Illustrations

What Causes Anxiety Disorders?

- The Anxiety Disorders Association of America states that anxiety disorders develop from a complex set of risk factors, including **genetics, brain chemistry, personality, and life events**.

- According to psychiatrist Carol W. Berman, as many as **50 to 75 percent** of individuals with panic attacks do not have an immediate family member who suffers from the disorder.

- Psychiatrist Jack M. Gorman states that someone's risk for panic disorder increases if he or she has suffered significant **emotional trauma** during childhood, such as the death of a parent or sexual/physical abuse.

- According to researcher Divya Mathur, the risk of developing social anxiety disorder for immediate familiy members of people suffering from the disorder is **10 times more** than for the general population.

- Scientists using **positron emission tomography** scans have found that function in some areas of the brain is different among people who have obsessive-compulsive order and those who do not.

- The National Institute of Mental Health states that evidence exists to show the connection between **genetics** and generalized anxiety disorder.

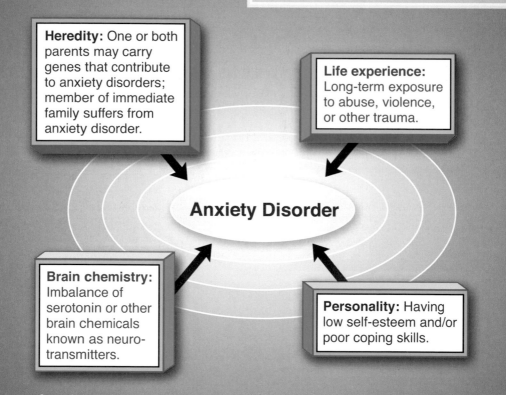

A Cluster of Causes

Medical researchers believe that anxiety disorders have multiple causes. Genetics, brain chemistry, life experiences, and personality have all been identified as possible contributors to anxiety disorders.

Heredity: One or both parents may carry genes that contribute to anxiety disorders; member of immediate family suffers from anxiety disorder.

Life experience: Long-term exposure to abuse, violence, or other trauma.

Anxiety Disorder

Brain chemistry: Imbalance of serotonin or other brain chemicals known as neuro-transmitters.

Personality: Having low self-esteem and/or poor coping skills.

Source: University of Maryland Medical Center, "Anxiety Disorders—Causes," February 5, 2008. www.umm.edu.

- An estimated **25 percent** of people who suffer from obsessive-compulsive disorder have an immediate family member who also has the disorder.

- According to the National Anxiety Foundation, scientists have discovered a link between obsessive-compulsive disorder and the brain chemicals **serotonin and dopamine**.

The Connection Between Abortion and Anxiety Disorders

Research has clearly shown that life experiences are one of the factors that can contribute to the development of anxiety disorders, and this proved to be true in a study published in 2008. It involved nearly 8,100 participants and examined associations between a history of abortion and a variety of mental health problems. The researchers found that women who had abortions had a significantly higher risk of developing one or more anxiety disorders, as this graph illustrates.

Percentage of women with each anxiety disorder based on abortion history

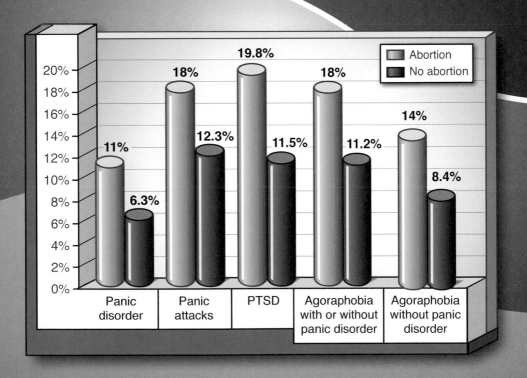

Source: Priscilla K. Coleman et al., "Induced Abortion and Anxiety, Mood, and Substance Abuse Disorders: Isolating the Effects of Abortion in the National Comorbidity Survey," *Journal of Psychiatric Research*, November, 2008. pp. 1–7.

Not All Trauma Survivors Get PTSD

People who suffer from post-traumatic stress disorder have endured some kind of traumatic experience such as war, kidnapping or rape, a horrific accident, or natural disaster. Yet according to the National Institute of Mental Health, most people who live through traumatic events do not develop PTSD. This diagram shows the risk factors that potentially lead to the disorder, as well as the resilience factors that help reduce the risk of developing it.

Risk factors for PTSD

Living through dangerous events and traumas
Having a history of mental illness
Getting hurt
Seeing people get hurt or killed
Feeling horror, helplessness, or extreme fear
Having little or no social support after a traumatic event
Dealing with extra stress after the event, such as loss of a loved one, pain and injury, loss of a job, and/or loss of a home

Resilience factors that may reduce the risk of PTSD

Seeking out support from other people such as friends and family
Finding a support group after a traumatic event
Feeling good about one's own actions in the face of danger
Having a coping strategy, or a way of getting through the bad event and learning from it
Being able to act and respond effectively despite feeling fear

Source: National Institute of Mental Health, *Post-Traumatic Stress Disorder*, 2008. www.nimh.nih.gov.

- The Anxiety Disorders Association of America states that **rape** is the most likely trigger of post-traumatic stress disorder; **65 percent** of men and **45.9 percent** of women who are raped will develop PTSD.

- Some studies suggest that **coffee and other stimulants** activate central nervous system pathways that cause panic attacks.

- Studies of fraternal and identical twins suggest that hereditary factors determine about **40 percent** of the risk for panic attacks.

- One theory about panic attacks is that they are caused by a **falsely activated alarm system** in a part of the brain known as the locus coeruleus.

What Are the Effects of Anxiety Disorders?

66For millions of people . . . anxieties and fears are over-whelming and persistent, often drastically interfering with daily life. These people may be suffering from anxiety disorders, a widespread group of psychological disorders that can be terrifying and crippling.99

—UCLA Anxiety Disorders Research Center, which seeks to further understanding of the factors that place people at risk for developing anxiety disorders and to develop more effective treatments.

66Anxiety disorders can be incredibly crippling.99

—Jennifer Hartstein, supervising psychologist at the Child and Family Institute at St. Luke's–Roosevelt Hospital in New York City.

Like all teenagers, Emily Ford yearned to be popular with her class-mates, to be invited to parties and dances and shopping trips to the mall, and to be part of the in-crowd the way she had been only a few years before. But no longer was she the bubbly, outgoing girl who was constantly surrounded by friends. She began to doubt herself constantly. She fretted over her appearance, was consumed with dread over having to read aloud in class, and agonized over what people thought of her. She writes: "Though I desperately wanted to be on top of everything, perfection proved impossible. I simply couldn't be the top student academically, athletically, musically, aesthetically, and socially. I was crushed to realize that many of my girlfriends were more fashionable, more athletic, better artists, better spellers, faster in math, and preferred by the boys in our class."[46] Although Ford did not know it at the time, she was losing her grip on reality and beginning a slow, painful descent into the abyss of social anxiety disorder.

Far Beyond Teenage Angst

Feeling anxious is just part of being a teenager. During the teenage years kids are going through numerous changes, from frustrating mood swings to figuring out who they are and what they want to do with their lives. It can be a difficult time, and it is perfectly natural for teens to feel stressed out and overwhelmed.

But those who suffer from social anxiety disorder experience feelings that are not typical or normal. These kids suffer—a lot. They are plagued with doubts that rob them of any shred of confidence or self-worth, and fear is their constant companion. Ford can certainly relate to this. She recalls waking up one morning when she was in the eleventh grade, sick at heart about her constant state of misery, dreading yet another day at school where she felt like a nobody. "Please, God, please let this be the day I'm different," she begged in the privacy of her bedroom. Realizing that was probably "asking too much," she rephrased her plea: "At least, please don't let this be the day when everyone finds out I'm crazy."[47]

> During the teenage years kids are going through numerous changes, from frustrating mood swings to figuring out who they are and what they want to do with their lives.

Despite her burning desire to get past the fears and feel like a normal teenager, Ford's condition worsened. Totally at the mercy of her crippling disorder, she sat in chemistry class one day and mentally tortured herself over what her former friends might be thinking about her. "The imagined thoughts of my classmates bombarded me from all sides," she writes. "'Her hair is so ugly.' 'Yeah, but did you see those yellow teeth?' 'Look at what she's wearing.' 'She's covered in cat hair.' 'She's covered in her own hair. Did you see her arms?' 'She better not be my lab partner.'"[48] That was just one of many agonizing days for Ford—and it was indicative of the rest of her time in high school.

By the time Ford's senior year had come to an end, she had given up all social activities, including participating in clubs and going to Friday night dances. She had abandoned her dream of a career in theater and quit both band and chorus. Because of the fears that now ruled her life, she was the only student in her class who did not fly to Disney World for the senior trip. Still, she continued to sink deeper and deeper into despair. "The more I avoided, the worse my social anxiety became," she writes. "Rather than risk blatant rejection, it seemed easier to believe that I was unable to be liked and incapable of fitting in. Allowed to grow freely, untested by real-world experiences, my fears quickly mushroomed out of control."[49]

> When the word *panic* is used in a sentence, the speaker may be referring to feeling "panicked" about not being prepared for a final exam, being stopped by a police officer for speeding, or having to face angry parents after getting home long after curfew.

Caught in the Grip of Panic

When the word *panic* is used in a sentence, the speaker may be referring to feeling "panicked" about not being prepared for a final exam, being stopped by a police officer for speeding, or having to face angry parents after getting home long after curfew. Yet even though these situations may incite what seems like panic, the feeling is temporary—and that is very different from the emotional turmoil of people with panic disorder. Their panic is constant, relentless, and terrible, so much so that it dominates their lives and renders them powerless to fight it. Some become so consumed with hopelessness that they turn to alcohol and drugs to escape their problems, even though using these substances does not really allow them to escape at all.

Joseph McGinty Nichol became intimately familiar with such feelings when he was 15 years old and started having panic attacks. They struck suddenly, without warning, and he was terrified because he had no idea what was happening to him. He writes:

> The worst part? They had no triggers. Totally random. A wave of panic would wash over me, and my heart would pound so fast that I couldn't tell one beat from another. Sometimes I would hyperventilate so hard that my limbs would go numb and I'd pass out. Sometimes the attacks were so overwhelming that the thought of dying was comforting. That's not a punch line. It's the truth.[50]

As terrible as Nichol's panic attacks were as a teenager, that was only the beginning of his struggle with panic disorder.

By the time Nichol was 18, he had grown accustomed to living in a constant state of dread. Fear consumed him and seemed to be in control of his very existence. He writes:

> Imagine your whole world getting smaller as the problem takes on a more agoraphobic expression. You stop going more than 10 miles away from your supposed "safe zone." And your safe zone isn't safe at all; you've just figured out how to tolerate the anxiety there. It wasn't, "Hey, I'm afraid of getting on a plane or a freeway or an elevator." I had a fear of everything. I had a fear of myself. The trauma, the embarrassment, the shame: Add it all up and it's just a . . . horrible experience that I couldn't talk about with anyone. I felt like less of a man.[51]

Finally Nichol got fed up. This was no way to live and he was done with it. He vowed to take control, get treatment for his panic disorder, and conquer his fears once and for all.

Today Nichol, who goes by the nickname McG, is a successful movie producer and director. Both *Charlie's Angels* movies were among the numerous films he has directed, and his most recent film, *Terminator Salvation*, tallied more than $372 million in box office sales. Despite his professional accomplishments and his triumph over panic disorder, Nichol knows that the disorder still lingers beneath the surface. He writes: "I'd never be so bold as to say, 'I'll never suffer from that again—it's over.' I have to be diligent even though I'm doing well. It's alive in me. It's who I am."[52]

Trauma's Agonizing Toll

People who have gone through traumatic events such as war, violent assaults, horrific accidents, or devastating natural disasters may be haunted for years after the incidents occurred. Painful memories can resurface at any time, making the person feel as though he or she is living through the trauma all over again. For some, this manifests itself in the form of post-traumatic stress disorder, a crippling condition that can devastate people's lives.

This was the unfortunate fate of a woman who was raped when she was 25 years old and who talked about the terrible aftereffects of the experience with the National Institute of Mental Health. "For a long time, I spoke about the rape as though it was something that happened to someone else," she says. "I was very aware that it had happened to me, but there was just no feeling." After doing her best to bury the terrifying memories of the violent incident, the woman began to have flashbacks. "They kind of came over me like a splash of water. I would be terrified. Suddenly I was reliving the rape. Every instant was startling. I wasn't aware of anything around me, I was in a bubble, just kind of floating. And it was scary. Having a flashback can wring you out."[53]

> People who have gone through traumatic events such as war, violent assaults, horrific accidents, or devastating natural disasters may be haunted for years after the incidents occurred.

Another PTSD sufferer is P.K. Philips, who was also the victim of a violent crime. As a child Philips was physically, emotionally, and sexually abused, and as a young woman she was raped at knifepoint. She says she was never the same after that and felt as though there was no safe place for her to go, including her own home. She describes the traumatic impact this had on her life:

For months after the at-
tack, I couldn't close my
eyes without envision-
ing the face of my at-
tacker. I suffered horrific
flashbacks and night-
mares. For four years
after the attack I was
unable to sleep alone
in my house. I obses-
sively checked windows,
doors, and locks. By age
17, I'd suffered my first
panic attack. Soon I be-
came unable to leave my

> " **Whether they suffer from extreme social anxiety, severe panic attacks, haunted memories of past trauma, or overwhelming obsessions, people with anxiety disorders know what it is like to live with misery.** "

apartment for weeks at a time, ending my modeling career abruptly. This just became a way of life.[54]

Years passed, and because Philips had few or no symptoms, she began
to think that her nightmare with PTSD was over. Then another traumatic incident occurred, and she says "it was as if the past had evapo-
rated,"[55] leaving her feeling as though she were back at the site of the
attack. Finally she was diagnosed with PTSD, and after finding out that
it was a real illness, as well as treatable, she began to think that she might
have a chance at a normal life.

Trapped in a Web of Fear

Living with severe obsessive-compulsive disorder can be horrible, making
those who suffer from it feel trapped in a constant state of despair from
which they see no escape. Some eventually reach the point where they
would rather die than go on living with such unbearable pain day after
day. Ed Zine understands this well because he suffered from one of the
worst cases of OCD that psychiatrists had ever observed.

After struggling with OCD for years, Zine's condition deteriorated
until he became totally disabled. He was incapable of working, going
out with his friends, or even talking to anyone face-to-face, because his
fears were just too overwhelming. He lived in the basement of his father's

home for nearly a year and only left the safety of his room to get food that his family left for him outside the door. Zine shares how the disorder nearly ruined his life, and he describes its devastating effects on those who struggle with it:

> OCD is just a word, but when it sucks the life out of my life, it also sucks the life out of my loved ones' lives. It is ruthless in its attack. When it hits you, it will not stop. We know that we are acting crazy, but we also know that we are not crazy. And while the outside world tries to take care of us, and reassure us, OCD spits in their faces, and tries to change, dictate, and control the ones who bring us love and reassurance.[56]

No Way to Live

Whether they suffer from extreme social anxiety, severe panic attacks, haunted memories of past trauma, or overwhelming obsessions, people with anxiety disorders know what it is like to live with misery. Even after they understand what is wrong with them and learn ways to work through their problems, many are never totally at peace with themselves or with life. P.K. Philips is one of the fortunate ones, as she explains: "For me there is no cure, no final healing. But there are things I can do to ensure that I never have to suffer as I did before. . . . I'm no longer at the mercy of my disorder."[57]

What Are the Effects of Anxiety Disorders?

66 A panic attack involves such a high level of anxiety that the person affected feels as if he or she can't breathe, is having a heart attack, going insane, or losing control. 99

—David L. Ginsberg, foreword to *100 Questions and Answers About Panic Disorder*, by Carol W. Berman. Sudbury, MA: Jones and Bartlett, 2010.

Ginsberg is a clinical associate professor in the Department of Psychiatry at New York University School of Medicine.

66 Many adults trivialize the torture each school day brings to so many. It's hard for some to recognize that a teenager can suffer from disabling social anxiety that is much more substantial than an occasional bout of test anxiety or a tongue-tied request for a date to the prom. 99

Emily Ford, *What You Must Think of Me*. New York: Oxford University Press, 2007.

Ford, who has suffered from social anxiety disorder since she was a child, is now involved in mental health consumer advocacy in Washington, D.C.

* Editor's Note: While the definition of a primary source can be narrowly or broadly defined, for the purposes of Compact Research, a primary source consists of: 1) results of original research presented by an organization or researcher; 2) eyewitness accounts of events, personal experience, or work experience; 3) first-person editorials offering pundits' opinions; 4) government officials presenting political plans and/or policies; 5) representatives of organizations presenting testimony or policy.

Primary Source Quotes

❝There are individuals with posttraumatic stress disorder who can be profoundly depressed and feel hopeless and despondent. And they certainly can have serious suicidal thoughts.❞

—Joan Anzia, "How Can I Tell When Thoughts of Harming Myself or Others Are Serious Enough to Get Professional Help?" ABC News, February 27, 2008. http://abcnews.go.com.

Anzia is an associate professor of psychiatry and behavioral sciences at Northwestern University.

❝Some individuals have anxiety symptoms that are so severe that they are almost totally disabled.❞

—Ronald M. Doctor, Ada P. Kahn, and Christine Adamec, *The A to Z of Phobias, Fears, and Anxieties.* New York: Checkmark, 2008.

Doctor is a psychology professor at California State University, and Kahn and Adamec are authors who specialize in health and medical issues.

❝Panic disorder is often accompanied by other serious conditions such as depression, drug abuse, or alcoholism and may lead to a pattern of avoidance of places or situations where panic attacks have occurred.❞

—Grace Tsai, "Panic Disorder," Discovery Health, 2010. http://health.discovery.com.

Tsai is a psychologist who writes about a variety of mental health issues.

❝Agoraphobia is usually thought to be the most crippling phobic disorder and simple phobia the least.❞

—Association for Behavioral and Cognitive Therapies, "Phobia," July 2007. www.abct.org.

The Association for Behavioral and Cognitive Therapies is committed to behavioral, cognitive, and other evidence-based principles to assess, prevent, and treat human disorders.

❝For millions of people in the United States, the anxiety does not go away, and gets worse over time. They may have chest pains or nightmares. They may even be afraid to leave home.❞

—National Institute of Mental Health, "Anxiety," February 11, 2010. www.nlm.nih.gov.

The National Institute of Mental Health seeks to reduce mental illness and behavioral disorders through basic and clinical research.

❝Panic attacks can greatly interfere with your life—and perhaps even endanger you or others.❞

—Mayo Clinic, "Panic Attacks and Panic Disorder," March 25, 2010. www.mayoclinic.com.

The Mayo Clinic is a world-renowned medical facility that is headquartered in Rochester, Minnesota.

❝It is true that very often having an anxiety disorder can disrupt relationships and lead to marital problems.❞

—Barbara Rothbaum, "Are People with an Anxiety Disorder More Likely to Have Marital Problems or Get Divorced?" ABC News, February 27, 2008. http://abcnews.go.com.

Rothbaum is director of the Trauma and Anxiety Recovery Program and a professor of psychiatry at Emory University.

What Are the Effects
of Anxiety Disorders?

- The Anxiety Disorders Association of America states that people with an anxiety disorder are **six times more likely** to be hospitalized for psychiatric disorders than those who do not suffer from anxiety disorders.

- Studies have shown that anxiety disorders are often **accompanied** by other mental health problems such as major depression and alcohol or substance abuse.

- According to research psychiatrist William R. Yates, chronic anxiety may be associated with increased risk for **cardiovascular disease**.

- The National Institute of Mental Health states that **post-traumatic stress disorder** is often accompanied by one or more other anxiety disorders.

- According to psychiatrist Jack M. Gorman, the most serious complication of generalized anxiety disorder is the onset of **major depression**, which most people with the disorder will suffer unless they are diagnosed and treated.

- The National Anxiety Foundation states that it is common for people with obsessive-compulsive disorder also to suffer **from clinical depression, panic attacks**, or both.

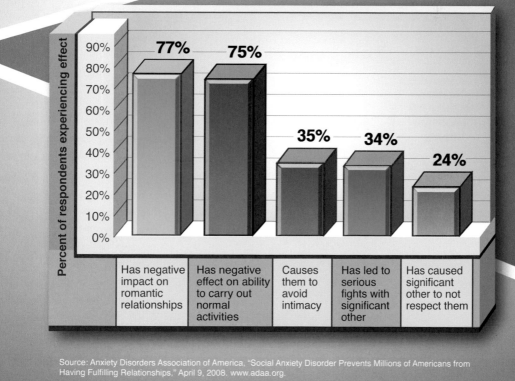

Impaired Quality of Life

People with social anxiety disorder experience fear and dread of social situations, sometimes to the point of total incapacitation. A survey conducted in April 2008 shows the profound effect the disorder has on people's social interactions and overall quality of life.

Effects of social anxiety disorder

Source: Anxiety Disorders Association of America, "Social Anxiety Disorder Prevents Millions of Americans from Having Fulfilling Relationships," April 9, 2008. www.adaa.org.

- Panic disorder is also associated with **migraine headaches, irritable bowel syndrome, asthma** and other chronic respiratory diseases, and increased risk for cardiovascular disease.

Companion Mental Illness

An April 2007 survey by the Depression and Bipolar Support Alliance surveyed people who suffer from bipolar disorder or depression and anxiety disorders. Participants shared their thoughts about how this combination of mental illnesses affects their lives.

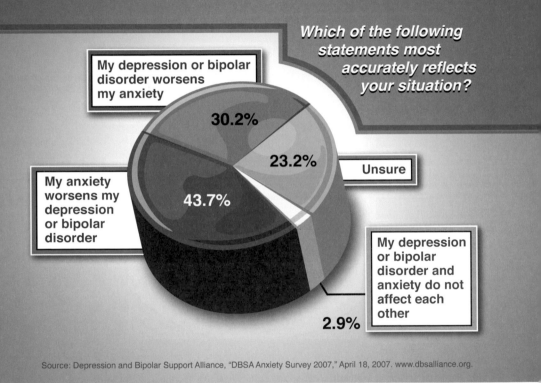

Which of the following statements most accurately reflects your situation?

My depression or bipolar disorder worsens my anxiety

30.2%

23.2%

Unsure

My anxiety worsens my depression or bipolar disorder

43.7%

My depression or bipolar disorder and anxiety do not affect each other

2.9%

Source: Depression and Bipolar Support Alliance, "DBSA Anxiety Survey 2007," April 18, 2007. www.dbsalliance.org.

- According to psychiatrist Sy Atezaz Saeed, the risk of depression is about **two to four times higher** in persons suffering from social anxiety disorder than for the general population.

- Psychiatrist Jack M. Gorman states that people with panic disorder have a high risk of developing depression, and when they do, they face an increased **risk of suicide**.

- According to physicians Jill Fenske and Thomas Schwenk, more than **50 percent** of people with OCD have suicidal thoughts, and **15 percent** have attempted suicide.

- According to David Veale, who is a psychiatrist in the United Kingdom, the family of someone with obsessive-compulsive disorder may become so involved in the person's **rituals** that they suffer greatly because of it.

- Psychiatrist Jack M. Gorman states that if panic disorder is not identified after the first attack, the condition can become **extremely debilitating**.

Can People Overcome Anxiety Disorders?

"Fortunately, anxiety disorders are treatable and the vast majority of people with an anxiety disorder can be helped with the right professional care."

> —UCLA Anxiety Disorders Research Center, which seeks to further understanding of the factors that place people at risk for developing anxiety disorders and to develop more effective treatments.

"The day may come when psychiatrists can wipe out phobias at will, like erasing a whiteboard. Who knows?"

> —Lev Grossman, a journalist from New York City who suffers from a phobia of being near people who are eating or drinking.

After years of suffering from agoraphobia, Fiona Bradshaw has finally begun to see pinpoints of light in the darkness. Through treatment, she has learned about the paralyzing fears that have plagued her for so long. She also understands that she is not yet free of them, and may never be completely free of them. She writes: "Many books and many therapists later I think I have a handle on what handles me. I know what happens to me when I panic, I know why it happens. Still, when it creeps over me I always seem to fold because it is so brutally terrifying."[58]

Bradshaw acknowledges that even with the progress she has made, she still has a long way to go. She often becomes frustrated, and she says that some days she feels as though she is chasing ghosts. Yet she is hopeful that with enough effort and hard work, she will eventually overcome her disorder and get her life back. "My method so far has been medication and talk therapy," she writes. "And in the talking I have come face to face with some of the ghosts. They make me want to run home and hide under the covers but I'm determined to face them at least. . . . I am determined to join ranks with the 'normals' but to also take with me what I've learned along the way."[59]

Incurable but Treatable

Unlike many diseases that can be treated with antibiotics or prevented with vaccinations, the same is not true for anxiety disorders. They are mental, rather than physical illnesses, so they cannot be cured in the traditional sense. As psychologist John M. Grohol writes:

> Cure is what doctors do for a broken wrist or scurvy. Set the wrist or give the patient a vitamin C shot, and voila! Done. Treating mental illness rarely results in a "cure," per se. What it does result in is a person feeling better, getting better, and eventually no longer needing treatment (in most cases). But even then, rarely will a professional say, "Yes, you're cured of your depression."[60]

Many people who undergo treatment for anxiety disorders can overcome them and go on to live normal, healthy lives. One success story is P.K. Philips, who, after battling severe anxiety for more than three decades, was relieved when she was finally diagnosed with PTSD. She no longer had to feel like she was crazy—she knew what she suffered from was a real mental illness. She writes: "I cannot express to you the enormous relief I felt when I discovered my condition was real and treatable. I felt safe for the first time in 32 years." Philips underwent therapy and took medications, and she says the treatment changed her life and

> **Unlike many diseases that can be treated with antibiotics or prevented with vaccinations, the same is not true for anxiety disorders.**

she is happier and more hopeful than she has been in a very long time. As she explains: "The world is new to me and not limited by the restrictive vision of anxiety. It amazes me to think back to what my life was like only a year ago, and just how far I've come."[61]

Triumphing over Trauma

Another PTSD survivor is Megan Krause, a staff sergeant with the U.S. Army who was stationed in Afghanistan and also did two tours in Iraq. As a medic, Krause witnessed firsthand the unspeakable horrors of war. She tended to innumerable wounded soldiers and agonized over those whose lives she was not able to save. Finally, when her last tour of duty ended and she returned home in 2006, Krause thought she had left the combat zone behind. She describes her homecoming: "I ran to my mother in that hangar; we both cried tears of joy. I told her it was over and I was fine. Boy, was I wrong."[62]

After getting settled and enrolling at Penn State University, Krause began to experience a great deal of stress at the many changes that were taking place in her life—and it was not long before the terrifying nightmares began. She had vivid dreams of explosions and saw the faces of fellow soldiers she could not save. Haunted by these memories, she began drinking heavily in a futile attempt to escape from the pain, and she started having suicidal thoughts. Then Krause says she hit rock-bottom: "It was when I found myself face down in the mud pit, in the middle of a pigpen . . . running from the insurgents that I thought were chasing me, that I realized I had not yet survived. I might not have been having suicidal ideations, but I was well on my way to killing myself."[63]

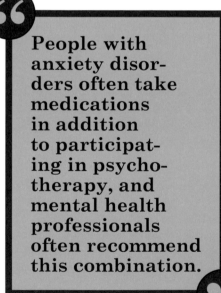

People with anxiety disorders often take medications in addition to participating in psychotherapy, and mental health professionals often recommend this combination.

Krause knew that she could no longer go on without help. She reached out to people in her reserve unit, who provided the support and encouragement that she needed. She was admitted to a veterans hospital, where she was diagnosed with PTSD, and she completed a treatment program in which she learned to face her psychological pain and work through it. Today Krause counsels others in the military who have also been stricken with PTSD. "I'm winning the battle with PTSD," she tells them, "and you can too."[64]

Treatment That Works

People with anxiety disorders often take medications in addition to participating in psychotherapy, and mental health professionals often recommend this combination. The National Institute of Mental Health explains: "Medication will not cure anxiety disorders, but it can keep them under control while the person receives psychotherapy."[65] The type of drug that is recommended varies based on the individual patient and the disorder that is being treated. Antidepressants, which in the past were reserved to treat depression, have proved to be effective for many types of anxiety disorders because they alter brain chemistry. Some of the most widely used are SSRIs, which can help restore the brain's serotonin levels to normal.

One type of therapy that has been immensely successful in treating people with anxiety disorders is known as cognitive behavioral therapy, or CBT. Working with a therapist who is trained in CBT techniques, patients recognize what their problem is and then devise very specific steps that will help them overcome the symptoms. Psychologist Judith S. Beck explains:

> In contrast to other forms of psychotherapy, cognitive therapy is usually more focused on the present, more time-limited, and more problem-solving oriented. Indeed, much of what the patient does is solve current problems. In addition, patients learn specific skills that they can use for the rest of their lives. These skills involve identifying distorted thinking, modifying beliefs, relating to others in different ways, and changing behaviors.[66]

Beck's reference to identifying distorted thinking is a key aspect of CBT. For instance, this type of therapy can help people with panic disorder understand that their panic attacks are a symptom of their disorder and are not life-threatening like heart attacks or cancer. People who suffer from phobias often learn that their fears are irrational and not based in reality. Those with OCD learn ways to challenge the validity of their obsessional thoughts so they no longer feel the need to perform compulsive rituals. Social anxiety disorder sufferers can change their thinking patterns so they no longer believe that others are watching and judging them.

Emily Ford is living proof that CBT can help someone with social anxiety disorder. After undergoing intensive therapy, along with taking medications, Ford was able to conquer her paralyzing fears and get on with her life. She writes: "At times, I get discouraged when I backslide a little or find that my progress is going more slowly than I would like. Then I remind myself that Rome wasn't built in a day, and neither was my personality. It took me 27 years to get to this point, and it's okay if it takes me a few more days, weeks, or even months to reach the next milestone." Ford acknowledges that she may never be fully rid of her anxiety disorder, but she does not plan to let it control her life anymore. "Social anxiety is, and perhaps always will be, a factor in many of my decisions, but it doesn't dictate my life. I no longer define myself solely in terms of social anxiety disorder." [67]

> " CBT can help people with panic disorder understand that their panic attacks are a symptom of their disorder and are not life-threatening like heart attacks or cancer. "

Facing Down the Dread

A type of CBT known as exposure-based therapy has achieved excellent results with many people who suffer from anxiety disorders. At the root of the therapy is the fact that patients who suffer from the disorders are consumed with fear, and by facing their fears head-on they can eventually learn to overcome them. Facing their fears, however, can be unbearably painful for many, because being confronted with the things that they fear the most is terrifying.

Yet this direct confrontation of fear is an important step in helping anxiety disorder sufferers heal because it helps them break unhealthy habits that they have developed as a result of their fears. For example, people who are plagued by fear and dread often do everything possible to avoid the source of their fear. In reference to people with PTSD, psychologist Matthew Tull explains:

> When a person experiences a traumatic event, he may begin to act in ways to avoid threatening situations with the goal of trying to prevent that traumatic experience from happening again. In many ways, this avoidance is a safety-seeking or protective response. However, as this avoidance behavior becomes more extreme, a person's quality of life may lessen. He may lose touch with family or experience difficulties at work or in relationships.[68]

One anxiety disorder that has achieved a very high success rate with exposure-based therapy is OCD, and this was shown in a study published in January 2008. Researchers from the OCD program at the University of California–San Diego obtained positron emission tomography scans of 10 OCD patients before they underwent four weeks of daily exposure-based therapy and after they had completed it. The second scans showed significant decreases in cellular activity in the areas of the brain that are known to be involved with the development of OCD. Specifically, they showed significant decreases in areas that are involved in appraisal and suppression of negative emotions. Sanjaya Saxena, who was the lead researcher for the study, says that the findings could have important implications for people who have OCD. He explains: "This study is exciting because it tells us more about how cognitive-behavioral therapy works for OCD and shows that both robust clinical improvements and changes in brain activity occur after only four weeks of intensive treatment."[69]

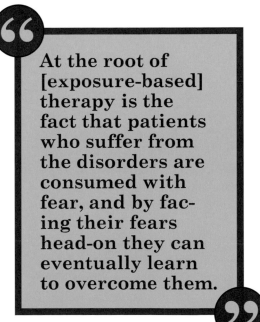

At the root of [exposure-based] therapy is the fact that patients who suffer from the disorders are consumed with fear, and by facing their fears head-on they can eventually learn to overcome them.

A Tough Battle

There are numerous success stories about people who have fought the battle with anxiety disorders and won. Yet there are also many who, for whatever reason, never seek treatment and therefore have little hope of getting better. Joseph McGinty Nichol (McG) is one of the survivors. He worked hard to overcome his panic disorder, and in the process, he got his life back. Nichol offers some words of wisdom for people who suffer from an anxiety disorder and desperately want to overcome it as he did: "Everyone has to deal with his ball and chain. Are you going to let it take you to the bottom, or are you going to figure out a way to carry on with it? Or will you cut yourself free of it? It requires fight and focus, but that's what defines us. . . . Throw down, find the courage to face what's going on, and move forward to eradicate it. That's real growth. That's real adulthood."[70]

Can People Overcome Anxiety Disorders?

66 Few people with social anxiety disorder seek professional help. For most patients suffering in silence, it remains a pervasive disabling condition that prevents them from leading a fuller, richer life. 99

—Divya Mathur, "The Neurobiology of Social Anxiety Disorder," Brain Blogger, April 22, 2010. http://brainblogger.com.

Mathur is a researcher who holds a PhD in molecular biology.

66 Not all people suffering from mental disorders are as fortunate as panic attack patients, who usually have such a good prognosis. In the cases of schizophrenia or obsessive-compulsive disorder, for example, there is a much lower rate of successful treatment. 99

—Carol W. Berman, *100 Questions and Answers About Panic Disorder*. Sudbury, MA: Jones and Bartlett, 2010.

Berman is a clinical instructor of psychiatry at New York University Medical School.

* Editor's Note: While the definition of a primary source can be narrowly or broadly defined, for the purposes of Compact Research, a primary source consists of: 1) results of original research presented by an organization or researcher; 2) eyewitness accounts of events, personal experience, or work experience; 3) first-person editorials offering pundits' opinions; 4) government officials presenting political plans and/or policies; 5) representatives of organizations presenting testimony or policy.

Primary Source Quotes

66There is help for people with panic disorder. In fact, it is one of the most treatable anxiety disorders.99

—National Institute of Mental Health, *When Fear Overwhelms: Panic Disorder*, 2008. www.nimh.nih.gov.

The National Institute of Mental Health seeks to reduce mental illness and behavioral disorders through basic and clinical research.

66All too often, people mistake these disorders for mental weakness or instability. The social stigma attached to mental illness often prevents those with anxiety disorders from asking for help.99

—Health Canada, "Mental Health—Anxiety Disorders," *It's Your Health*, July 2009. www.hc-sc.gc.ca.

Health Canada is the Canadian government's principal public health agency.

66Identification and effective treatment of childhood anxiety disorders can decrease the negative impact of these disorders on academic and social functioning in youth and their persistence into adulthood.99

—Sucheta D. Connolly and Sonali D. Nanayakkara, "Anxiety Disorders in Children and Adolescents," *Psychiatric Times*, October 8, 2009. www.psychiatrictimes.com.

Connolly and Nanayakkara are psychiatry professors at the University of Illinois–Chicago.

66A great deal of research is now going on to identify further risk factors for anxiety disorders in our genes and our early experiences. Ultimately we may be able to prevent the conditions from arising.99

—Jack M. Gorman, "Anxiety and Panic—the Dana Guide," Dana Foundation, June 2009. www.dana.org.

Gorman is a professor and vice-chair for research in the Department of Psychiatry at Columbia University in New York City.

66 There is hope for individuals with anxiety disorders, because these problems can be effectively treated with cognitive therapy and behavior therapy. 99

—Association for Behavioral and Cognitive Therapies, "Anxiety Disorders," September 2007. www.abct.org.

The Association for Behavioral and Cognitive Therapies is committed to behavioral, cognitive, and other evidence-based principles to assess, prevent, and treat human disorders.

66 Up until a few years ago we did not have effective treatments for OCD. New medications and behavior therapy now give many patients significant relief. 99

—National Anxiety Foundation, "Interesting Facts About OCD," 2009. www.lexington-on-line.com.

The National Anxiety Foundation is an organization that seeks to educate the public about anxiety through printed and electronic media.

66 There is currently no proven drug treatment for specific phobias, but sometimes certain medications may be prescribed to help reduce anxiety symptoms before someone faces a phobic situation. 99

—University of Maryland Medical Center, "Mental Health: Specific Phobia," February 5, 2008. www.umm.edu.

A teaching hospital located in Baltimore, the University of Maryland Medical Center provides a full range of health care to people throughout Maryland and the mid-Atlantic region.

Can People Overcome Anxiety Disorders?

- The Anxiety Disorders Association of America states that even though treatment for anxiety disorders is often successful, only about **one-third** of people suffering from one or more of these disorders undergo treatment.

- Health Canada states that the most common form of treatment for anxiety disorders is a combination of **drug therapy** and **cognitive behavioral therapy**.

- A 2007 survey by the Anxiety Disorders Association of America showed that **36 percent** of people with social anxiety disorder reported experiencing symptoms for 10 or more years before seeking help.

- Psychiatrist Jack M. Gorman states that relapse rates after someone with an anxiety disorder stops taking medication are high, between **30 and 40 percent**.

- According to the National Institute of Mental Health, **panic disorder** is one of the most treatable of all anxiety disorders.

- The Anxiety Disorders Foundation states that antidepressant medications have been found to reduce symptoms of obsessive-compulsive disorder by as much as **30 to 50 percent** in most individuals.

Medications and Psychotherapy Are Both Effective

Although most people who suffer from anxiety disorders never seek treatment, those who do often see a significant improvement in their quality of life. A *Consumer Reports Health* survey published in July 2010 examined the types and effectiveness of treatment for depression, anxiety, or both.

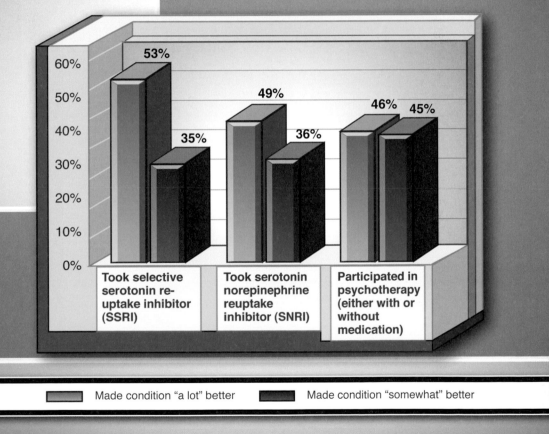

Made condition "a lot" better · Made condition "somewhat" better

Source: *Consumer Reports Health*, "Depression and Anxiety," July 2010. www.consumerreports.org.

- According to Health Canada, because anxiety disorders have some **biological basis**, the most common drugs prescribed are antidepressants and antianxiety drugs.

Medication Side Effects

Medication is often part of treatment for anxiety disorders. These drugs help alleviate symptoms and often make people feel better, but some are known to have side effects.

Medication	Disorder	Possible side effects
Antidepressants; selective serotonin reuptake inhibitors (SSRIs) or serotonin norepinephrine reuptake inhibitors (SNRIs)	Depression, panic disorder, OCD, PTSD, social anxiety disorder, generalized anxiety disorder	Temporary nausea and/or jitters. Some studies have suggested that these drugs increase the risk of depression and suicidal thoughts, especially in young people
Tricyclic antidepressants	OCD, generalized anxiety disorder	Dizziness, drowsiness, dry mouth, weight gain
Benzodiazepines (antianxiety drugs)	Social anxiety disorder, generalized anxiety disorder, panic disorder	Dizziness, drowsiness, upset stomach, blurred vision, headaches, confusion, grogginess, nightmares
Beta-blockers	Anxiety disorders that involve physical symptoms such as trembling and sweating	Fatigue, cold hands, dizziness, weakness

Sources: National Institute of Mental Health, *Mental Health Medications*, 2008. www.nimh.nih.gov; National Institute of Mental Health, *Anxiety Disorders*, 2009. www.nimh.nih.gov.

- According to psychiatrist Carol W. Berman, each new patient with panic attacks has a **90 percent** chance of becoming attack free within in a month after treatment begins.

Cognitive Behavioral Therapy and OCD

Mental health professionals widely agree that the best type of therapy for people with obsessive-compulsive disorder (OCD) is cognitive behavioral therapy (CBT). To determine the effectiveness of CBT in children with OCD, researchers studied three groups; one whose members underwent 12 sessions of CBT over a 14-week period, another whose members started CBT but did not finish, and a third group who completed family-based relaxation therapy rather than CBT. This graph shows the progress made by the groups after the study was concluded.

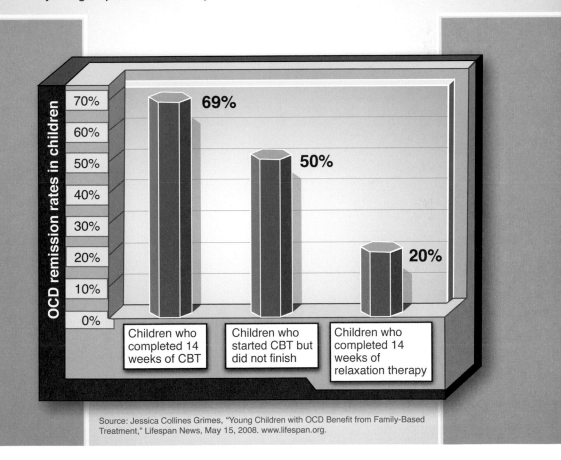

Source: Jessica Collines Grimes, "Young Children with OCD Benefit from Family-Based Treatment," Lifespan News, May 15, 2008. www.lifespan.org.

- The Anxiety Disorders Foundation states that in patients with post-traumatic stress disorder, cognitive behavioral therapy has consistently achieved success rates of about **70 percent**.

- According to the National Institute of Mental Health, **alcoholism and depression** sometimes have such a strong effect on someone with an anxiety disorder that treating the disorder must wait until the other conditions are brought under control.

- Studies suggest that early treatment of anxiety disorders can **prevent complications** such as depression, while delay of treatment can worsen a sufferer's prognosis.

Key People and Advocacy Groups

Anxiety Disorders Association of America: An advocacy group that is dedicated to the prevention, treatment, and cure of anxiety disorders.

Anxiety Disorders Foundation: An organization that seeks to improve the lives of everyone who is affected by anxiety disorders.

Aaron Tempkin Beck: An American psychiatrist who is known as the father of cognitive behavioral therapy.

Steven J. Brodsky: A well-known clinical psychologist from New York who specializes in cognitive behavioral therapy for obsessive-compulsive disorder, phobias, and panic disorder.

National Alliance on Mental Illness: An advocacy group that is dedicated to improving the lives of people who suffer from mental illness, as well as the lives of their families.

National Anxiety Foundation: An organization whose goal is to educate the public about anxiety disorders.

National Institute of Mental Health: A government agency that seeks to reduce mental illness and behavioral disorders through research and that supports science that will improve the diagnosis, treatment, and prevention of mental disorders.

Jerilyn Ross: Known as a visionary leader in the field of mental illness, Ross was among a small group of doctors and patients who founded the Phobia Society of America in 1980 (the name was later changed to the Anxiety Disorders Association of America).

Chronology

1789

American physician and author Benjamin Rush publishes an article in which he defines a phobia as "a fear of an imaginary evil, or an undue fear of a real one."

1895

Austrian neurologist Sigmund Freud publishes an article that earns him considerable recognition and establishes anxiety neurosis as a psychiatric classification.

1879

In his book *The Pathology of Mind*, British psychiatrist Henry Maudsley introduces the word *panic* into psychiatry when he describes panic attacks.

1952

The first edition of the American Psychiatric Association's *Diagnostic and Statistical Manual of Mental Disorders* is published, ushering in the formal classification of mental illnesses.

1800   **1900**   **1950**   **1980**

1871

In the classic paper "Die Agoraphobie," German neurologist Carl Friedrich Otto Westphal describes three male patients who suffer from extreme dread when entering streets or public places. Westphal is the first to use the term *agoraphobia* to describe this disorder.

1966

British psychologist Victor Meyer reports that two cases of obsessive-compulsive disorder have responded to a behavioral therapy technique that later becomes known as exposure and response prevention.

1970s

A group of psychiatrists begins using the term *post-Vietnam syndrome* to describe a delayed reaction to combat that includes anger, depression, alienation, and sleeplessness. This later becomes known as post-traumatic stress disorder.

1883

William Hammond, who cofounded the American Neurological Association, coins the term *mysophobia* to describe an obsessive fear of contamination.

1968

The second edition of the American Psychiatric Association's *Diagnostic and Statistical Manual of Mental Disorders* defines *social phobia* as a specific fear of social situations or an excessive fear of being observed and/or scrutinized by others.

1980

The third edition of the American Psychiatric Association's *Diagnostic and Statistical Manual of Mental Disorders* brings major changes in the classification of anxiety disorders, with the inclusion of panic disorder, post-traumatic stress disorder, and generalized anxiety disorder.

2010

Researchers from the Netherlands announce a study showing that anxiety disorders may increase the risk of heart attack, stroke, heart failure, and death in people with heart disease.

1989

To address the needs of veterans with military-related post-traumatic stress disorder, Congress mandates the creation of the National Center for PTSD as an agency of the U.S. Department of Veterans Affairs.

2003

In experiments with mice, researchers from Case Western Reserve University discover a gene that regulates levels of a chemical responsible for controlling anxiety, impulsive violence, and depression in humans.

1980   1995   2010

1985

Psychiatrist Michael Liebowitz and clinical psychologist Richard Heimberg advocate for aggressive research on social phobia, which is so misunderstood that many mental health professionals call it the "neglected anxiety disorder."

1994

In the fourth edition of the American Psychiatric Association's *Diagnostic and Statistical Manual of Mental Disorders*, obsessive-compulsive disorder is included as a diagnosis, and the term *social phobia* is replaced by *social anxiety disorder*.

2002

Spanish geneticist Xavier Estevill discovers that a gene on some other chromosome, or an environmental factor early in development, may cause an abnormality of chromosome 15, which may make some people more susceptible to panic attacks.

1990

The Phobia Society of America, founded in 1980, changes its name to Anxiety Disorders Association of America.

1999

Canadian medical scientist Jacques Branwejn announces that he and his colleagues have discovered a genetic mutation that appears to put people at risk for panic attacks.

Related Organizations

American Psychological Association (APA)

50 First St. NE

Washington, DC 20002-4242

phone: (202) 336-5500; toll-free: (800) 374-2721

Web site: www.apa.org

The APA is a scientific and professional organization that represents psychology in the United States. A topic search on its Web site produces a number of publications about anxiety disorders, including symptoms, effects, and treatment options.

Anxiety Disorders Association of America (ADAA)

8730 Georgia Ave.

Silver Spring, MD 20910

phone: (240) 485-1001 • fax: (240) 485-1035

Web site: www.adaa.org

The ADAA is dedicated to the prevention, treatment, and cure of anxiety disorders and to improving the lives of people who suffer from them. Its Web site features numerous publications that define anxiety disorders and discuss topics such as symptoms, treatment, and research.

Anxiety Disorders Foundation

PO Box 560

Oconomowoc, WI 53066

phone: (262) 567-6600 • fax: (262) 567-7600

e-mail: info@anxietydisordersfoundation.org

Web site: www.anxietydisordersfoundation.org

The Anxiety Disorders Foundation is dedicated to improving the lives of everyone who is affected by anxiety disorders. Although its Web site does not feature an abundance of information, several informative articles about anxiety disorders are available.

Association for Behavioral and Cognitive Therapies (ABCT)

305 Seventh Ave., 16th Floor

New York, NY 10001

phone: (212) 647-1890 • fax: (212) 647-1865

Web site: www.abct.org

The ABCT is committed to the advancement of a scientific approach to the understanding and improvement of problems that affect human health. Its Web site offers fact sheets, news articles, and a variety of publications.

Freedom from Fear

308 Seaview Ave.

Staten Island, NY 10305

phone: (718) 351-1717 • fax: (718) 980-5022

e-mail: help@freedomfromfear.org

Web site: www.freedomfromfear.org

Through advocacy, education, research, and community support, Freedom from Fear seeks to have a positive effect on the lives of people who suffer from anxiety, depression, and related disorders. Its Web site provides detailed information about anxiety disorders, a mental health resource library, and a link to the Freedom from Fear blog.

Health Canada

Brooke Claxton Building, Tunney's Pasture

70 Colombine Driveway

Ottawa, ON K1A 0K9

phone: (613) 957-2983 • fax: (613) 952-7747

Web site: www.hc-sc.gc.ca

Health Canada is the Canadian government's principal public health agency. Its Web site's search engine produces numerous publications about health-related issues, including information about anxiety disorders.

International Association of Anxiety Management

e-mail: editor@anxman.org • Web site: www.anxman.org

The International Association of Anxiety Management is a comprehensive Web-based resource for those who suffer from anxiety disorders. A wealth of information may be found on its site, including facts about the main types of anxiety disorders, frequently asked questions, and an online forum.

Mental Health America

2000 N. Beauregard St., 6th Floor

Alexandria, VA 22311

phone: (703) 684-7722; toll-free: (800) 969-6642 • fax: (703) 684-5968

Web site: www.nmha.org

Mental Health America is dedicated to helping people live mentally healthier lives and educating the public about mental health and mental illness. Its Web site features an "Anxiety Disorders: What You Need to Know" section, as well as fact sheets, information about medications and clinical trials, and information developed for military families.

National Alliance on Mental Illness (NAMI)

3803 N. Fairfax Dr., Suite 100

Arlington, VA 22203

phone: (703) 524-7600; toll-free (800) 950-6264 • fax: (703) 524-9094

Web site: www.nami.org

The NAMI is dedicated to improving the lives of people who suffer from mental illness, as well as the lives of their families. Its Web site features fact sheets, news releases, online discussion groups, and a search engine that produces numerous articles about anxiety disorders.

National Anxiety Foundation

3135 Custer Dr.

Lexington, KY 40517-4001

phone: (859) 272-7166

Web site: www.lexington-on-line.com/naf.html

The National Anxiety Foundation's goal is to educate the public about anxiety disorders. Its Web site features information about types of anxiety disorders, causes, treatment options, and suggestions for further research.

National Institute of Mental Health (NIMH)

Science Writing, Press, and Dissemination Branch

6001 Executive Blvd., Room 8184, MSC 9663

Bethesda, MD 20892-9663

phone: (301) 443-4513; toll-free: (866) 615-6464 • fax: (301) 443-4279

e-mail: nimhinfo@nih.gov • Web site: www.nimh.nih.gov

The NIMH seeks to reduce mental illness and behavioral disorders through research and supports science that will improve the diagnosis, treatment, and prevention of mental disorders. Its Web site features statistics, archived *Science News* articles, and a search engine that produces numerous publications about anxiety disorders.

University of California–Los Angeles Anxiety Disorders Research Center

Department of Psychology

Franz Hall—Box 951563

Los Angeles, CA 90094-1563

phone: (310) 206-9191 • fax: (310) 825-9048

e-mail: adrc@psych.ucla.edu • Web site: http://anxiety.psych.ucla.edu

The Anxiety Disorders Research Center seeks to further understanding of the factors that place people at risk for developing anxiety disorders and to develop more effective treatments. Its Web site provides detailed descriptions of the main anxiety disorders as well as information about current studies and treatment methods.

For Further Research

Books
Jeff Bell, *Rewind, Replay, Repeat: A Memoir of Obsessive-Compulsive Disorder*. Center City, MN: Hazelden, 2007.

Carol W. Berman, *100 Questions and Answers About Panic Disorder*. Sudbury, MA: Jones and Bartlett, 2010.

Ronald M. Doctor, Ada P. Kahn, and Christine Adamec, *The A to Z of Phobias, Fears, and Anxieties*. New York: Checkmark, 2008.

Charles H. Elliott and Laura L. Smith, *Overcoming Anxiety for Dummies*. Indianapolis: Wiley, 2010.

Emily Ford, *What You Must Think of Me*. New York: Oxford University Press, 2007.

Tom Metcalf and Gena Metcalf, eds., *Phobias*. Detroit: Greenhaven, 2009.

Allen R. Miller, *Living with Anxiety Disorders*. New York: Facts On File, 2008.

Michael A. Tompkins and Katherine A. Martinez, *My Anxious Mind: A Teen's Guide to Managing Anxiety and Panic*. Washington, DC: Magination, 2009.

Periodicals
J. Ross Baughman, "Anguish of Story Can Haunt Journalists," *Washington Times*, April 17, 2009.

Michelle Burford, "High Anxiety," *Essence*, March 2009.

Benedict Carey, "Extinguishing the Fear at the Roots of Anxiety," *New York Times*, July 11, 2008.

GP, "Clinical: Phobias," May 21, 2010.

Lev Grossman, "Why Overcoming Phobias Can Be So Daunting," *Time*, January 11, 2010.

Barbara Kantrowitz, "Help for Panic Attacks," *Newsweek*, June 25, 2008.

Jeremy Katz, "Are You Crazy Enough to Succeed?" *Men's Health*, July/August 2008.

Kathleen Kingsbury, "Stigma Keeps Troops from PTSD Help," *Time*, May 1, 2008.

Jeffrey Kluger, "When Worry Hijacks the Brain," *Time*, August 13, 2007.

Emily Listfield, "Fumbling Toward . . . Looking Out for . . . Diving into . . . Dreading . . . Feeling My Way to 40," *Redbook*, May 2009.

Julia McKinnell, "Swim Class for the Truly Terrified," *Maclean's*, July 20, 2009.

Bob Meadows and Caroline Howard, "Living in Fear," *People*, September 8, 2008.

Joe Posnanski, "Zack Greinke Is in Total Control," *Sports Illustrated*, May 4, 2009.

Roxanne Patel Shepelavy, "Extreme Stress," *Good Housekeeping*, April 2009.

Raj Thakkar, "Clinical: The Basics—Anxiety," *GP*, June 12, 2009.

Liz Welch, "Get Happier Guide," *Self*, May 2010.

Internet Sources

Shahreen Abedin, "Seeing Crash Reports Can Worsen Flying Phobia," CNN, February 13, 2009. www.cnn.com/2009/HEALTH/02/13/flying.phobia.crashes/index.html.

Health Canada, "Mental Health—Anxiety Disorders," *It's Your Health*, July 2009. www.hc-sc.gc.ca/hl-vs/alt_formats/pacrb-dgapcr/pdf/iyh-vsv/diseases-maladies/anxiety-anxieux-eng.pdf.

Robert L. Leahy, "Anxiety Files: Do You Have Panic Disorder?" blog, *Psychology Today*, April 10, 2010. www.psychologytoday.com/blog/anxiety-files/200904/do-you-have-panic-disorder.

National Institute of Mental Health, *Anxiety Disorders*, 2009. www.nimh.nih.gov/health/publications/anxiety-disorders/nimhanxiety.pdf.

ScienceDaily, "A Little Anxiety Is Sometimes a Good Thing," April 5, 2008. www.sciencedaily.com/releases/2008/04/080403104350.htm.

Social Anxiety Network, "Social Anxiety: The Largest and Least Understood Anxiety Disorder." www.social-anxiety-network.com.

Source Notes

Overview

1. Merely Me, "Writing About Anxiety: A Personal Perspective," Health Central Anxiety Connection, January 6, 2010. www.healthcentral.com.
2. Merely Me, "Writing About Anxiety."
3. George Pratt, "If I Have Suffered from an Anxiety Disorder, Am I Likely to Continue to Experience Anxiety or Will It Go Away?" ABC News, February 27, 2008. http://abcnews.go.com.
4. Health Canada, "Mental Health—Anxiety Disorders," *It's Your Health*, 2009. www.hc-sc.gc.ca.
5. Quoted in Lindsay Anderson, "The Struggle Within/On Edge," *Battalion*, April 3, 2008. http://media.www.the batt.com.
6. Quoted in Alexandra Jacobs, "Finding Her Voice," *Allure*, April 2010, p. 188.
7. OCD Chicago, "What Causes OCD?" 2010. www.ocdchicago.org.
8. Lev Grossman, "Why Overcoming Phobias Can Be So Daunting," *Time*, January 11, 2010, p. 45.
9. National Institute of Mental Health, *Anxiety Disorders*, 2009. www.nimh.nih.gov.
10. Charles S. Mansueto, "OCD and Tourette Syndrome: Re-examining the Relationship," Obsessive-Compulsive Foundation, Winter 2008. www.ocd chicago.org.
11. Anxiety Disorders Association of America, "Understanding Anxiety Is the First Step in Getting Your Life Back," 2010. www.adaa.org.
12. Anxiety Disorders Association of America, "Understanding Anxiety Is the First Step in Getting Your Life Back."
13. Jack M. Gorman, "Anxiety and Panic—the Dana Guide," Dana Foundation, June 2009. www.dana.org.
14. Merely Me, "Writing About Anxiety."
15. Quoted in Carol W. Berman, *100 Questions and Answers About Panic Disorder*. Sudbury, MA: Jones and Bartlett, 2010, p. v.
16. National Institute of Mental Health, *Anxiety Disorders*.
17. Grossman, "Why Overcoming Phobias Can Be So Daunting."
18. Irene Wielawski, "What to Ask About Anxiety," *New York Times*, July 11, 2008. http://health.nytimes.com.
19. Patrick B. McGrath, *The OCD Answer Book*. Naperville, IL: Sourcebooks, 2007, p. 125.
20. Grossman, "Why Overcoming Phobias Can Be So Daunting."
21. Grossman, "Why Overcoming Phobias Can Be So Daunting."
22. National Institute of Mental Health, *Anxiety Disorders*.

What Are Anxiety Disorders?

23. Quoted in Dagobert D. Runes, ed., *The Selected Writings of Benjamin Rush*. New York: Philosophical Library, 1947, p. 220.
24. Quoted in Runes, *The Selected Writings of Benjamin Rush*.
25. Quoted in Runes, *The Selected Writings of Benjamin Rush*.
26. HealthyPlace, "Symptoms of Anxiety," October 2, 2008. www.healthy place.com.
27. National Institute of Mental Health, *Anxiety Disorders*.
28. Quoted in *On the Media*, "The Art of Diagnosis," listener comments, National Public Radio, December 26, 2008. www.onthemedia.org.

29. Quoted in *On the Media*, "The Art of Diagnosis."
30. Quoted in Berman, *100 Questions and Answers About Panic Disorder*, p. vi.
31. Quoted in Sarah Spendiff, "Agoraphobia: What's Going On in My Head?" *Independent*, February 2, 2009. www.independent.ie.
32. Ronald M. Doctor, Ada P. Kahn, and Christine Adamec, *The A to Z of Phobias, Fears, and Anxieties*. New York: Checkmark, 2008, p. xi.
33. Doctor et al., *The A to Z of Phobias, Fears, and Anxieties*, p. xi.
34. Quoted in Michiko Kakutani, "Recalling a Literary Family, and Phobias," *New York Times*, January 30, 2007. www.nytimes.com.
35. Quoted in Jeremy Katz, "Are You Crazy Enough to Succeed?" *Men's Health*, July–August 2008, p. 150.
36. Jeff Bell, "Living with OCD," video, CBS News, June 10, 2009. www.cbsnews.com.
37. Cathy Frank, "How Is 'Normal' Anxiety Different from an 'Anxiety Disorder'?" ABC News, February 27, 2008. http://abcnews.go.com.

What Causes Anxiety Disorders?
38. Mayo Clinic, "Anxiety: Causes," June 29, 2010. www.mayoclinic.com.
39. Sheryl Ankrom, "The Human Brain: How Brain Cells Communicate with Each Other," About.com: Panic Disorder, February 1, 2009. http://panicdisorder.about.com.
40. Anxiety Disorders Association of America, "Medication," 2010. www.adaa.org.
41. Quoted in Don Rauf, "SPECT Identifies Possible Basis of Social Anxiety Disorder," Diagnostic Imaging, June 5, 2008. www.diagnosticimaging.com.
42. Quoted in *Harvard Gazette*, "Gene Variants Probably Increase Risk for Anxiety Disorders," March 6, 2008. http://news.harvard.edu.
43. Stacey Kuhl-Wochner, "Social Anxiety/Social Phobia Research," blog, OCD Center of Los Angeles, November 6, 2009. www.ocdla.com.
44. Cathy Frank, "What Causes an Anxiety Disorder?" ABC News, February 27, 2008. http://abcnews.go.com.
45. Quoted in Caroline Cassels, "Susceptibility to PTSD, Anxiety, Depression Hereditary," Medscape Today, December 22, 2008. www.medscape.com.

What Are the Effects of Anxiety Disorders?
46. Emily Ford, *What You Must Think of Me*. New York: Oxford University Press, 2007, p. 22.
47. Ford, *What You Must Think of Me*, p. 26.
48. Ford, *What You Must Think of Me*, p. 27.
49. Ford, *What You Must Think of Me*, p. 36.
50. Quoted in Mike Zimmerman, "Scared and Pissed Off," *Best Life*, May 2009, p. 112.
51. Quoted in Zimmerman, "Scared and Pissed Off," p. 112.
52. Quoted in Zimmerman, "Scared and Pissed Off," p. 112.
53. Quoted in National Institute of Mental Health, *Anxiety Disorders*.
54. P.K. Philips, "My Story of Survival: Battling PTSD," Anxiety Disorders Association of America, 2010. www.adaa.org.
55. Philips, "My Story of Survival."
56. Quoted in Terry Weible Murphy, *Life in Rewind*. New York: HarperCollins, 2009, p. 234.
57. Philips, "My Story of Survival."

Can People Overcome Anxiety Disorders?

58. Quoted in Spendiff, "Agoraphobia."
59. Quoted in Spendiff, "Agoraphobia."
60. John M. Grohol, "How Do You Cure Mental Illness?" blog, Psych Central, May 22, 2009. http://psychcentral.com.
61. Philips, "My Story of Survival."
62. Quoted in U.S. Army Reserve, "'Real Warrior' Describes Post-traumatic Stress," 2010. www.usar.army.mil.
63. Quoted in U.S. Army Reserve, "'Real Warrior' Describes Post-traumatic Stress."
64. Quoted in U.S. Army Reserve, "'Real Warrior' Describes Post-traumatic Stress."
65. National Institute of Mental Health, *Anxiety Disorders*.
66. Judith S. Beck, "Questions and Answers About Cognitive Therapy," Beck Institute. www.beckinstitute.org.
67. Ford, *What You Must Think of Me*, pp. 120–21.
68. Matthew Tull, "Exposure Therapy for PTSD," About.com: Post Traumatic Stress (PTSD), December 17, 2008. http://ptsd.about.com.
69. Quoted in ScienceDaily, "Rapid Effects of Intensive Therapy Seen in Brains of Patients with Obsessive-Compulsive Disorder (OCD)," January 22, 2008. www.sciencedaily.com.
70. Quoted in Zimmerman, "Scared and Pissed Off," p. 112.

List of Illustrations

Index

Note: Boldface page numbers refer to illustrations.

About the Author

Peggy J. Parks holds a bachelor of science degree from Aquinas College in Grand Rapids, Michigan, where she graduated magna cum laude. An author who has written nearly 100 educational books for children and young adults, Parks lives in Muskegon, Michigan, a town that she says inspires her writing because of its location on the shores of Lake Michigan.